WHAT WHAT WHAT

Lauren Goodwin

Cover art by Caroline Hein

Printed by CreateSpace in the United States of America

ISBN-10: 1986075621
ISBN-13: 978-1986075626

For any questions or comments, please contact
whatwhatwhatbook@gmail.com

To my family, extended and immediate. Your love for me is written in the pages of this book. Without it, they would be blank. Thank you.

"Love takes up where knowledge leaves off."

-Saint Thomas Aquinas

CONTENTS

Author's Note

The quest I have committed myself to is the search for truth. If I am being honest, everybody is searching for truth. It is why we love reading—to find out what happens to beloved characters. It is why we love watching television shows, especially crime shows—to find the outcome of a dire situation. (It is also why Netflix is so popular; why wait a week for a new episode when you can find out the truth in an hour?) The quest for truth has been driving humanity for the better half of forever and it is the only journey that proves itself to be timeless.

My quest for truth has followed me in every endeavor, even when I didn't know it. It derives from my need-to-know mentality. I hate being in the dark about anything that's going on around me. It can be positive and negative. I learn a lot, but it also leads to a tendency to gossip, something that I've been trying to avoid, many times unsuccessfully, in my high school life.

The search for truth can be in something as simple as what multiple choice answer to bubble in on a big test to the purpose of one's very own existence. Truth has been debated upon in politics, philosophy, theology, and even something as concrete as science. Maybe this is why it enthralls me so much—that I can partake in something so much bigger than myself, something so far over my head, yet so deceivingly basic.

The book that follows is my quest for truth up until this point. I am young and have a lot of truth to discover, uncover, and deny. I don't have it figured out, but I don't think anybody does either. The quest for truth would be pointless if there was none. The only thing we have to do is keep chipping away at that big block of the unknown until we get there, and we will, but probably not in this lifetime. Even though I have not lived a lot of life yet, the first, young years serve a purpose in my quest for truth. The essays you are about to read pertain to what I know, what I don't know, and what I think I know. All three different stages are equally as important to finding the truth. I decided to title this book What What What because it expresses the confusion that surrounds us, even when we are certain of the truth. There is so much we don't know, and the haunting word "What" follows us everywhere we go, begging us to uncover it a little more.

There are many questions young people face throughout childhood and their inevitable transition into adulthood. What am I doing? What am I going to do? Where am I going to go? Why am I doing it? All these questions are addressed in my essays, but never answered.

I tell many family stories and experiences from my childhood. I write them to help me figure out what they mean, and how they contribute to who I am. My memory isn't perfect, just like every other human, so I tell these stories how I remember them and hope it is true to the original. For the sake of privacy, some names are changed. I know that many of the people in my life have grown since I've seen them; my goal is not to embarrass them, but to show you my growth and their part in it. For this reason, I disguise their true name.

I embrace confusion with all its caveats and flaws because it is the state of wanting to know more. The following essays follow memories, aha moments, faith struggles and friend struggles, each leading me into some sort of unknown. My never-ending quest for truth is never complete without the abundance of "What" questions. Here are some of them. Enjoy.

-Lauren Goodwin

1. The Robot Disciple

Throughout elementary and middle school, every Saturday morning from October to Easter, I sat in a classroom listening to a teacher talk about our Catholic faith and reading from the workbook we all had to learn from. The title of the class was CCD, an acronym which I never figured out until many years after taking the classes. Growing up, I learned that, usually, any combination of letters stood for something else, but no one could tell me what CCD meant, so I just accepted it. (This was before I had access to Google). Apparently, it stands for Confraternity of Christian Doctrine. What that means, I don't know. Essentially, it is a Sunday school for Catholic children who attend public school, but on Saturdays.

I took the classes at the private school attached to my parish, St. Joseph's. The classrooms were always cluttered with bright and engaging posters encouraging students to "Read!" or "Be Kind." The teacher's desk in the corner had all types of papers and notebooks scattered across it from the school week previous. Sometimes even a name plate sat on the end of the desk, keying us CCD students into what private school was like.

I didn't particularly enjoy CCD, mostly because I had to wake up early on Saturday mornings every week for some time. I was a natural learner, however, and could retain the lessons about Bible stories and miracles of Jesus. I was quick to answer questions when no one else raised their hands, probably because I loved to talk any chance I could get, but also to prove to the teacher that I knew the answer when no one else did. This became a trend, especially in my fourth-grade year, when my classmates gave me the nickname "Robot." They thought that since I knew so much about the lessons, the information must have been programmed into me. I had always wanted a nickname. Lauren was too basic, and you couldn't shorten it to make it sound better, but Robot was not what I was expecting. Sometimes when I answered a question correctly, I would hear a classmate whisper "Robot!" under his or her breath. I guess it's what I get for showing off.

Although the students in the class thought it was weird that I knew so much information, the teacher thought it was great. He was a Catholic convert, who entered the Church in his forties. He was kind and had a fatherly presence. He would let us play games that tested our knowledge on certain aspects of the Bible. One time we split into two teams, boys and girls, and had to search through the Bible to find out who the Son of David was. I knew it couldn't have been Jesus because he was the Son of Mary. We scoured scripture for about half an hour trying to find the answer until the boys blurted out, "It's Jesus! Jesus is the Son of David!" Lo and behold, they were right, and the teacher gave them a St. Michael medal as their prize. I had no idea what a medal was at that time, but I was still upset that I didn't get one.

Other than the odd nickname, fourth-grade CCD class gave me something that I am forever grateful for; knowledge that God was beyond an obligation. Religion was always something I was supposed to do, rather than cultivating a continuous relationship. I can't remember the first Mass I went to—it was always just there in my memory. Going to class was just another activity disrupting my Saturday morning. But that year, the class engaged my mind and showed me the real reason why I go to Mass in the first place. Although there was much I still had to learn, it was like someone had lit a match in my heart that year, the fire slowly encompassing me with a passion that I wouldn't fully discover until later.

It was also the first time I found out what the rosary was. To me, rosaries were just fancy necklaces that my grandmother would make and give to all the cousins every Christmas. Turns out, you actually use them to pray. Our teacher told us about how his daughter was marrying a man who thought all Catholics were evil and everything they said was false. He said he didn't want his daughter's future husband to think so badly of her religion. He decided that every day he would say a rosary so that his future son-in-law's heart would change. By the end of the story we were all on the edge of our seats wondering what happened to the guy or if his daughter ended up not marrying him. His daughter and the man did end up marrying each other, and the husband converted to Catholicism. My mouth hung open. Although my young mind probably exaggerated the story, it still astonishes me. How powerful could God be to turn someone hateful into someone who loved Him? I went home that day and dug through the drawers in my room, looking for one of the rosaries my grandmother had gifted me. I prayed it all the way through, probably forgetting the words to prayers and not even thinking about the mysteries that went along with it. I just wanted God to do something for me like he did for my teacher.

Later in the year, our teacher decided we deserved a break and said we could watch a movie during class. He gave us a choice between two different movies: one I can't remember, and the one we chose—a documentary about St. Joan of Arc. Next class he brought the movie in and we all crowded around the old TV hanging from one of the corners of the classroom and watched the story of Joan of Arc. My eyes never left the screen as I watched Joan carry out the duties given to her by St. Michael the Archangel, St. Margaret, and St. Catherine by fighting for the French in the 100 Years War. I watched as she escaped the Burgundians by jumping out of a seventy-foot tower, landing on the soft earth, unscathed. To my dismay, Joan was captured for the last time by the English and was burned at the stake for a heresy she did not commit. At the end of the movie, I was ready for whatever God wanted to throw at me. If He wanted me to fight like Joan, then I would. Seeing how Joan of Arc could accomplish so much at such a young age while being a woman fascinated me.

Everyone my age had someone they were obsessed with. I tried finding someone who I could look up to, but it changed every week, and eventually I would get bored of whatever singer or boy band I discovered. But I found St. Joan of Arc and better yet, she could do something for me. She could pray for me; after all, she is closer to God than I am. I held St. Joan in my heart for years, calling upon her when I was lacking confidence and thinking of what she would do if she were here. I held on to her until it was time for me to be confirmed. When young Catholics become old enough, they receive the last Sacrament of Initiation, which is confirmation as a full, adult member of the Catholic Church. When we begin, we take the name of a Saint to be our model throughout the process, and who could pray for us. There were many Christophers amongst the boys, who is the patron saint of sports, and Cecilias among the girls, the patron saint of music. I chose St. Joan of Arc, who I felt had already been my Confirmation Saint for a while. I finally took her name as a part of mine, and when I was confirmed in 2015, the Bishop spread holy oil across my forehead, sealing me with the Holy Spirit, and cementing my path towards God, with Joan as my guide.

Ever since that CCD class in fourth grade, I felt God pulling me towards Him every day, calling me to something greater than myself. Eventually, that led me to my church's youth group. I was in sixth grade. My mom saw an ad in my church bulletin for the middle school youth group and thought I should take a friend and see what it was all about. So, one Sunday night my Mom drove us to church, trying to find the youth center where the event was held. After a while we found a barn-looking building on the corner of the property and walked around until we found a sign on a door at the back end of the building. We walked through hesitantly, only to be greeted by a friendly face telling us to sign in.

There were couches everywhere in the room, and the cinder block walls were painted like it was in a Nickelodeon show. I was most excited about the soda and chips on top of the air hockey table, but didn't want to be the only one eating, so I sat on the couch with my friend and awkwardly gazed around the odd room until someone talked to us. One girl named Nicole, who was a volunteer at the Youth group, came up and talked to me while we were on the couch. She sat on the ground in front of me and we talked for at least thirty minutes. Or *I* talked for thirty minutes. If I went as far as opening my mouth, there was no stopping the endless stream of words that would tumble out. I could talk to anyone and anybody about anything, and I would do it for way too long. But Nicole still sat in front of me and listened, nodding as I kept on going. After just talking for a while, the youth minister led us in prayer, and we talked about the faith. Eventually, 8:30 had rolled around, and the youth minister announced that this was the last event of the summer, and she was leaving the position. I slumped in my seat. I was so excited for the next event, about all the people I could meet, and talking more to Nicole, but I had been too late. Although I was sad I had missed a whole summer of youth group, I still gushed about it to my mother on the way home, while my friend, on the other hand, wasn't so impressed.

About a year later I saw an ad in the church bulletin and decided to go back to youth group, this time by myself. It was the first of many events I would attend.

I kept going back every weekend until the end of eighth grade. It was at youth group where I wasn't the Jesus Kid, because everybody was a Jesus Kid. Not only did I laugh more, and talk more (still way too much), I learned so much. I would sit on those comfy couches while Lauren, the youth minister, would give talks about living out the faith and following Christ. We learned about different terms in the Church and how they related to Jesus, like the Hypostatic Union (which sounds completely different than what it actually is). We would also have thoughtful discussions about our doubts, insecurities, and questions where nothing was off limits. At youth group, I opened a book I had never even heard of before, full of information more valuable than anything I had known before. Youth group formally introduced me to the faith.

With the secular culture growing stronger, it is youth groups like mine that keep the faith alive, well, and young. Without the environment that my church had fostered in youth ministry, I would have never paid any attention to the faith that now fills me with joy—something society could never give me.

Although my first encounter with Youth Group was five years ago, my first (conscious) encounter with Christ happened a few years earlier, in that un-airconditioned elementary school classroom on early Saturday mornings. It is where I was met with the immature teasing of fourth-graders, but it is also where I saw compassion, in the form of a teacher, wanting me to grow. I saw compassion in Joan. She showed me her resilience and her unrelenting trust in God, but she also opened the gates to a new realm of possibility for a nine-year-old girl who had no idea what

God had in store for her.

2. Girl Scouts

In Kindergarten, I had my first glimpse into adulthood when I joined the Girl Scouts of America. It seems ironic, since the Girl Scouts is a quite juvenile organization where you sell cookies and exchange pins with other girl scouts called SWAPS, which stands for "Special Whatchamacallits Pinned Somewhere." Nonetheless, to my six-year-old self, being a girl scout was something of great nobility. I was mature. Every month, I was to attend Girl Scout troop *meetings*. To me, a meeting was something that important people would go to when they needed to discuss important things—only adults do that. When the troop leader told us that we would have these meetings, I felt important, powerful, and adult. When I couldn't have a play date with my friends because of Girl Scouts, I could tell them I have a *meeting* to attend. I felt just like my dad, who went to meetings at his job every day. I had a job like him now, except my meetings were at a local church instead of downtown Baltimore, and I wore a teal vest instead a suit.

Along with these important meetings came status. There were many different levels of being a girl scout and the more patches you got the higher you climbed on the ladder. I started out as a Daisy, then moved up to Brownie when I got all the patches needed. (When you're a Daisy, your patches are pastel petals of a flower that you iron on your vest until the flower is complete.) I don't remember much of being a Daisy, but I do remember the "bridge ceremony," where I gained my new brown Girl Scout vest and the esteemed title of "Brownie."

My career as a Girl Scout was filled with all kinds of "professional" experiences. I would go door to door selling boxes of cookies (which were only three dollars a box when I was a Girl Scout, a much fairer price, I think) to fund raise for our monthly trips. I'd walk up to my neighbors' doors, proudly sporting my vest and a big smile and ask them sweetly, "Would you like to buy a box of Girl Scout cookies?" Most of them would buy at least one or two. I even had a neighbor one year who bought ten whole boxes. My mom made me write her a thank you note for buying so many.

Once the cookies were in, I'd go with my mother in our golden Honda minivan to pick up the inventory from the house of one of my fellow Girl Scouts to deliver them to buyers. There were prizes for selling certain amounts of cookies, similar to a school fundraiser. I would try to get my parents and grandparents to buy more cookies than they would ever need just so I could get some of the fancy things that came with the highest sale. Whoever got the highest sales was given a patch to iron on to her vest, displaying the number she reached. Unfortunately, my parents are sane and didn't buy over twenty boxes of cookies just to satisfy my competitive nature. So, I didn't get the coveted patch saying I sold 100+ or 200+ boxes of cookies, but someone else did. Every year someone had to volunteer to have all the cookies delivered to her house. The same mom did it every year, and it was always her daughter who sold the most cookies. It only made sense that they stole cookies from someone else or marked other people's sales as their own. Although I was adamant about their dodgy practices, I never brought them to light, hoping that the next year I would get the exciting prize worth selling a thousand boxes of cookies.

Even though I didn't sell the most cookies, I still was proud to be called a Girl Scout. I had a job, a duty that I had to carry out. It was something many first graders didn't get to experience at that age. I was so proud of my title that on Boy Scouts day at school, where all the Boy Scouts would come in dressed in their uniforms, I came in dressed in my Girl Scout uniform. I was so excited to strut around school sporting my brown vest packed with patches displaying my achievement. But before I could even step into my first-grade classroom, another girl told me that it was Boy Scouts day, *not* Girl Scouts day. So, I shoved my brown vest into my backpack where no one would get to see how grown up I was.

Eventually, my career as a Girl Scout came to an end. After first grade was over, I was ready to continue my quest to sell the most cookies, but my best friend wasn't. We had joined Girl Scouts together and after about two years of doing it, she decided it was lame. So, for fear of being lame, I quit too.

Although Girl Scouts was a nice preview of what I

thought adulthood would look like, facing the real thing has turned me upside down. Becoming independent disguises itself as an exciting endeavor with freedom to do whatever you want because your parents aren't breathing down your neck. But as I get closer to leaving home and living on my own, the really ugly side of adulthood reveals itself. Adulthood comes with all kinds of decisions. Big ones like where to go to college or what career path to follow, to smaller ones like finding time to meet with friends and choosing a roommate. All these decisions have the same weight; all of it is completely foreign and unknown.

Although Girl Scouts was somewhat of a window into the future, my view wasn't exactly true to the real thing. In Girl Scouts, I know my purpose: to sell cookies. I knew where I was going. My mom would take me to all the events, tell me what to say, and how to act. The troop leaders organized all the fun events and got the cookies for us to be delivered. Now, faced with decisions that I've never had to make for myself before, the reality is much scarier—no box of cookies could have prepared me for it.

A teacher once told me that teenagers are at the best time in life to write horror stories. Not only are we unbelievably angsty but everything at this point in our lives is completely new. There is immense pressure at this stage in life to choose the right career that will take up every day of our lives for the rest of our life. It is like the cheesy horror movie where we yell to the main character not to enter the eerie closet, except when we turn eighteen, everyone has to go into that eerie closet and is expected to come out unscathed. When combined with all the things we don't know and all the things we think we know, reality becomes a whirlpool of confusion and fear.

Entering into adulthood can be synonymous with entering into the unknown. No matter how many self-help books we may read or advice we get from parents or grandparents, we still know almost nothing about what the real world will look like for us because it is different for everybody. It is why coming of age novels are so beloved by readers. They give us the wisdom that one character receives while maturing. Although I wish I could write about some profound experience where I found a way to skip the bumpy and unpleasant road to adulthood, I can't. There is still so much I don't know about adulthood, but I do know that the transition is not going to be pretty. In fact, the only possible road to adulthood is the bumpy, unpleasant road. And I am about to turn onto that road very soon.

My glimpse into adulthood as a Girl Scout has showed me what it feels like to have responsibility. Except in the adult world, I can't make a living off selling (now four dollar) boxes of cookies to neighbors and I also don't get patches to iron on to my clothes when I achieve something. Adulthood is very real, unlike the care-free organization of the Girl Scouts. It is very scary, and most of the time I don't even know what I don't know. There are many, many young people going through the same confusion as I am. Some may be franticly applying to any scholarship possible to pay for college. Others are still plagued with the question of whether they even want to go to college and face the pressure and scrutiny of parents and relatives. The transition into adulthood is universal yet individual. There is no one correct way to go about it. I guess the only way is to figure out as we go, hoping our early glimpses into adulthood will come in handy one day.

3. Camping Memoir #1

It was what we called "Camp Weekend," where we would all meet up at my grandfather's trailer for three days and there were no rules. It was Olivia and me, along with my cousins Kristen and Kelsey, and some of their family friends. It was only the fathers and daughters who went (with the exception of Nick, the lone son.) My grandfather's trailer was up on a mountain, surrounded by tall trees and no neighbors. On a late-August morning, Dad would wake my sister and me up to get ready to leave for my cousins' house. We always drove up with them and stopped at McDonald's for lunch on the way up, a first in the series of unhealthy meals throughout the weekend.

Once we pulled into the driveway of our cousins' house, we would pack our uncle's white Pilot full of all the camping necessities: air mattresses, sleeping bags, Martin's white bread, a big tub of Country Crock butter, mountain pie makers, bags of pepperoni, and foldable chairs to sit by the fire. After our visit to the local McDonald's, we drove all the way up to the campsite in the middle of nowhere. When we got close we'd turn onto a downhill gravel path, the car's wheels crunching over the little stones making me jump out of my seat; it meant we were there.

Once at the bottom of the tiny hill, there was a fire pit to the left, not touched since the year before. It was where we sat in our foldable chairs, cooking mountain pies, hot dogs, hamburgers, and bratwursts. Further towards the left was the trailer. The trailer wasn't that big, and I can't remember what the exterior looked like. I regret not taking a long look at it the last time we were there. There were two small steps leading up to the entrance on the side of the trailer. First, there was a kitchen, where the dads would make pancakes Saturday morning, and where all the old-fashioned candies that my grandparents brought sat on the counter, waiting to be eaten by all the sweet-toothed daughters. Next to the kitchen was a tiny bedroom, only a double sized bed fit inside of it. Anna and Morgan, the two oldest daughters, always slept there. Further down the hall, next to the bedroom was a small bathroom where all us girls would brush our teeth with a jug of water brought from home. (Sink water was supposedly undrinkable.) By the toilet, near the toilet paper, was a little handwritten sign that read, "If it's yellow let it mellow. If it's brown flush it down." It was a reminder to only flush when we really needed to, since there was no real septic system up where the trailer was, so conserving water was a must.

Then there was the room with the bunk bed in the back. This was where most of the daughters would sleep, as many as we could fit in the little bunk bed and an air mattress on the floor. I remember trying to sleep in that room every year, so I could be near the "big girls." That bunk was where we would stay if it rained, listening to music on our iPod Nanos, playing card games, and scratching words and phrases into the bottom of the top bunk, hoping that anyone who might stay in the trailer after us would know about our annual camp weekend.

A little way up from the trailer, hidden in the woods, was what we called the salamander pond. Emma, Nick, my sister Olivia, and I (we were the youngest at camp) would go there all the time on the hunt to catch salamanders with our bare hands or with the grimy nets that were at the trailer. We would scoop the nets into the dirty, murky water, hoping a bright green salamander would sit there wiggling his limbs. There was one elusive orange salamander amongst all the green ones. Nick got a hold of it one time and posed for a picture, holding it by the tail and letting it dangle before he dropped it to the ground.

Camp weekend was also called Yes weekend because whatever the daughters wanted, the dads would almost always say yes. You want soda with breakfast? Sure. Candy at 11:00 at night? Absolutely. Want to make a monstrous ten-foot fire that could possibly burn down the entire forest around us? Sounds fun. It was a mother's nightmare, which was why we didn't invite them.

One year, one of the dads, Mark, brought a neon green chain saw to camp called the "Wild Thing." Although it sounds like something we would make up, it was printed right there on the side, in purple shredded letters. When we ran out of firewood, he would rev it up and the trees behind the fire pit would meet the Wild Thing, falling to the ground and into the creek. The creek was another spot where we spend a lot of our time. We would make little houses out of the big slabs of stone and the clay in the little crannies on the side of the creek. When they took the Wild Thing to the trees, the creek would fill with saw dust, drying up the little streams of water, and covering the little homes we made.

One year we had a competition to see who made the best house. The teams were as follows: Emma, Nick, Olivia, and I; Kristen, Kelsey, Jenna, and Mia; Anna and Morgan. We worked all Saturday on our houses. Kristen even spent forever making a little person out of grass and twigs to sit in their house, only for it to be thrown into the fire later by Jenna. We forced the dads to judge our houses at the end of the day. Since they didn't want anyone's feelings to be hurt, they chose superlatives over first, second, and third place. I can't remember what they said ours was, probably because the superlatives were lame, and we wanted to win.

Another reason why camp was Yes weekend was because we could stay up however late we wanted. When it got dark the only lights were from the campfire and the trailer, leaving the gravel path up to the paved road completely pitch black. We played a game called chicken, where we had to run all the way up the gravel road in the pitch black without a flashlight and then run back down. It wouldn't help that Don, another one of the dads, would tell us a scary story before we had to go up to the road. If we weren't successful, we were deemed a chicken. We would also run around on the main road in front of the campground. Whenever a car would pass us by, we would run back as fast as we could to hide behind the trees surrounding the road. It was especially intense when we would play in the dark, and could detect the oncoming cars by their headlights, jumping behind the bushes and trees whenever someone would yell, "Car!"

Camp weekend was like a little hole in the year when everything was different. The only thing I brought with me from the real world was some family members and clothes. Everyone else I only saw that one weekend out of the whole year. Camp weekend was a constant—as I grew up many things about me changed, but every year I would go to camp. It didn't matter where it was. Eventually, it came time for my grandfather to sell the lot where his trailer sat, and our camp weekend setting changed. We moved to a campground, to a friend's cabin, and to a rented cabin in the succeeding years. Although we didn't have the salamander pond, or the wood-dust filled creek anymore, the unwavering annual trip continued without a hitch and I have never met another group of people who could have that much fun in any setting. The "yes" followed us wherever we went, letting us let out our reckless tendencies for one weekend of roughin' it. Camp took me out of time, out of the real world, and made me feel a part of something.

4. Growing Pains

One of the greatest perks about attending youth group every week is my stacked arsenal of games and icebreakers. If you're ever bored at a party or some other event, I'm your girl. At youth group, focus is put on everyone feeling welcome, so naturally, playing "get to know you" icebreakers or other silly games is a must at any and all events. At the high school events, everything typically goes smoothly, directions are followed, nothing breaks, and (mostly) everyone has fun. Middle school, however, quickly devolves into a mish mosh of screaming, falling, laughing, and any other noise that a twelve-year-old can produce. It's a symphony of chaos, that can only be stopped by the arrival of pizza and soda.

Learning everyone's names is a must when volunteering at youth group. I've come to know that there are a lot of people with the same name. My name is Lauren, along with the youth minister, another high schooler, and a middle schooler. There are also two Emily's, two Nicole's, and three Patrick's. With all the people who filter through youth group every week, no amount of name games can handle putting that many names to faces and faces to names. I used to be great at remembering people's names.

They would walk in, and I'd already be writing their name tag before they said "Hi." That was until I learned too many names and my brain couldn't handle another, so it kept deleting some to make room for the new ones. I slowly stopped offering my services to name-tag writing duty. Sometimes I wouldn't get so lucky, and when I wasn't sure if it was Natalie or Caroline walking through the door, I sneakily asked them to spell their name, my attempt at remembering their name without letting them know I forgot it.

Youth group attracted all kinds of people from different homes, backgrounds, and stories. Many were forced into the car by their parents, others were too excited to be there (I am the latter). But each is equally valued and important—if it were a youth group full of me's, you would have to hold your ears due to the sheer loudness; nobody would want that. The diversity of thought, interest, and just about everything else is what makes youth group so enjoyable.

Each night was different, a new topic, but more new people and new interactions. I would sit at the lopsided picnic table outside the youth center looking at the sketchbook of a quiet eighth grader, admiring the scratchy pen marks made by her talented hands. Other nights, if we got bored, two or three of the volunteers would break out Apples to Apples. The three of us would turn into ten all shoved together in a somewhat circle on the ground trying to come up with the most absurd combinations to win over whoever was the "judge."

There was a small room in the back of the youth center

painted a bright slime green with a ping pong table. Many games were won and lost, along with dented ping pong balls. Most of the time we would give up keeping score and use the chalkboard on the opposite wall to write "So-and-so was here" or our favorite Bible verses in colored chalk. If I was lucky, the air hockey table was open, and I could challenge anyone who thought they could take me on. The only problem was that the hockey table was right by the door to the staircase, leading to the upstairs room, and if anyone was walking down from getting pizza or going to the bathroom, they might have been met with an elbow to the stomach from the player winding up for a goal shot. It wasn't the most ideal placement, but it allowed enough room for two players and a few instigators who cheered on their friends.

Youth group gave me everything school couldn't. At school, pressure to seem "cool" was overwhelming, causing everybody to mask their real selves and worry if anyone thought they were weird. I was constantly reflecting on myself, wondering what I could change to make so-and-so like me more. This was the social pressure bubbling up every week, and I don't know what I would have done if I didn't have a place to explore who I really was, instead of who everyone else wanted me to be. Youth group wasn't just a place where we learned about God and played cheesy games all evening. The atmosphere was different. Every time I stepped in the room, my real self would emerge, desperately waiting to be revealed after a long week of navigating the social confusion of junior high. I looked forward to youth group every weekend, waiting at my door for my mom to come downstairs and take me there, my nervousness growing if we were even one minute late.

My leaders at youth group are arguably the best thing to ever enter my life. Not only did they give me an environment to simply grow, but they taught me about the God who loved me more than I could ever comprehend. How could I not be grateful for such a substantial contribution to my livelihood? They listened to me, something not many adults had ever done. Growing up as a kid with a loud mouth, I was always self-conscious about how much I talked, if I was too enthusiastic, or came off "too strong." They were the first to truly listen to what I had to say, and to teach me the value of words, and embrace my energy as if it were a gift, not to be controlled but to be used for God.

Youth group gave me stories and memories. Moments that made life sweeter. The kind you look back on and can't stop laughing even though it happened years ago. I look back on these memories, thinking about their purpose, how they impacted me. A lot of times I don't know. I don't know why they happen or why God put them in my life. I may not know their purpose, but I do know they have one—I feel the marks of those memories, the laughter, the excitement, knowing that something that good must mean something great. As I grow further away from these stories and memories, I pray I never forget them, for if I do, I will never know why such goodness came my way. I tell them, in hopes of deciphering their silliness, loveliness, and hopefulness.

. . .

Arguably the most attractive part and selling point of

youth group was the pizza every weekend. We'd have it delivered from Dominick's, a pizza place nearby that gave us a discount for some greasy, top-quality food. We ordered there every weekend, so they knew where to deliver always, which can be hard for anyone who doesn't know the St. Joseph campus, since the Youth Center looks more like an old barn behind the school that hasn't been used in a while. For a time when I was in middle school, we would always have a pizza delivery man named Matt, who looked almost identical to the stereotypical images of Jesus with the long hair and beard. It was uncanny; we knew it was the Lord telling us that eating all this pizza was okay. Every time he would knock on the door, we'd yell "Jesus!" One day, when youth minister Lauren was going to pay for the pizza, she asked Matt if he knew about his doppelganger.

"You know my kids call you Jesus? Have you ever gotten that before?" asked Lauren.

"Yeah, I have. But it means more coming from you guys," said Matt. Lauren came back and told us what he said, a series of "awes" ensuing after. Eventually, various pizza delivery guys came, and we heard rumors that Matt had cut his holy hair, but every once in a while when we hear the loud knock on the door, someone would remind us about how Jesus delivered our pizza every weekend.

The first half of youth group was reserved for a talk given by the youth minister and small group discussion. Small group can be meaningful and profound, even the middle school groups. Sometimes they speak words of wisdom that even catch the adult volunteers off guard; other times, however, we giggly teens with short attention spans would derail the conversations. One night, we were discussing how Jesus lived in the context of the era. This of course means discussing Jewish tradition, some of which middle schoolers are unfamiliar with. After some discussion about the time that Jesus lived in, some were still confused about how Jesus worshipped and praised.

"You know Jesus was Jewish, right?" said Lauren. Many kids nodded in agreement, some didn't quite understand how it was possible.

"What?" cried Tommy, a young sixth grader in the group. "You mean he didn't even believe in himself?" After suppressing laughs, Lauren clarified Tommy's confusion. Stories like these populated our conversations during events or retreats, reminiscing on our iconic moments together.

The youth center isn't our only home. Every year we went on a winter retreat to get away from school and our jam-packed schedules to focus on our relationship with Christ. We would go snow tubing at Ski Liberty, a resort near the Maryland/Pennsylvania border and then spend the rest of our time at a beautiful retreat center in Rockville. It was actually a Jewish retreat center, ironically, that graciously hosted us for the weekend. The retreat center is nicer than most hotels I have ever been in. We would share a room with one other person (I roomed with the other high schooler Lauren) and we'd each get a double-sized bed along with a bathroom *inside the room*, fully equipped with a shower. To anyone who has attended a youth group retreat, these are definitely luxurious accommodations. All of us were used to sleeping in squeaky bunk beds with only a sink to brush our teeth in, along with shared bathrooms at the end of the hall. There would rarely be air conditioning unless you were lucky and got a room with a window unit. When we would go to bigger conferences, we would stuff six girls in a dorm room meant for two and rush back to the communal bathroom after the last event, so we wouldn't wait until midnight to get a shower. The Jewish retreat center was a great break from roughing it at most places, and we also got to eat kosher for the weekend.

Retreats were what everyone looked forward to throughout the year. We would hold up signs before and after Mass smiling and advertising for our big spaghetti dinner fundraiser to raise as much as we could for the annual youth conference in Ohio or our winter snow tubing retreat, as well as our pizza fund for every weekend. The smiles from the church ladies were the best kind of donation, as well as the kids begging their parents to buy a ticket. Our fundraisers would often go off without a hitch; we'd have a cake wheel, raffles, and the most delicious Italian dinner. The cake wheel is always my favorite, not only because there is a chance to win cake, but also to see the parents of young children go down the wormhole of "just one more game." The raffle was fun too, but a stressful job. Our pastor, Father Kevin, would always market for it, running around the parish center in his naturally (very) loud voice yelling "Raffle tickets! Five bucks! They're coming around!" Father Kevin's advertising went over a little too well, resulting in me and my friend running around between tables sloppily collecting money and handing out tickets until there were no more left, hoping that we got to everyone who yelled "Over here!"

As I am writing this, it is my senior year of high school and my last year participating in the high school youth group. The youth center has received a much-needed renovation, and thus the bright green wall has been painted over. There are plans to get rid of the cozy furniture I once sat on when I first talked to Nicole in sixth grade. My closest friend just graduated (the other high school Lauren) and the Youth Minister Lauren has left St. Joseph to work part time and take care of her two young boys. We have a new pastor at St. Joseph, and my favorite Deacon was just assigned to a new parish in the Archdiocese. I've grown close with the new youth minister, Betsy. I went to conferences with her and helped at events and confirmation classes. I've heard her stories about college, growing up in Wyoming, playing Ultimate Frisbee (which I hear she is a beast at), and even sitting on the same stage as Pope Francis. Now, a great job opportunity has come her way and it is in New Jersey.

St. Joseph, my second home, has seen so much change. It is hard to see the place you love so much becoming so different than what it was when you found it. No matter what the change is—good or bad—getting used to it is hard. I've always been stubborn, and I don't like change even if it is good for me. Seeing all the people I love so dearly move on from St. Joe breaks my heart, since I am just not ready yet. My parents sometimes remind me that I am leaving in a few months, so all this change won't affect me long. The thought doesn't comfort me like it should. I can be selfish; I wish my home of St. Joseph could stay the same for me while I am gone, so when I come back from wherever I am, I can visit my home the same way I left it. Life doesn't work that way; change doesn't care what you want or who you are; it just happens.

Change hurts like growing pains. It's confusing, too. You can't exactly see what will come of it until it's happened. That's probably why I grapple with it so much. I like to be in control of my surroundings, to always know what is going on and what is going to happen. Giving up that control takes a whole lot of guts for me and I just haven't gotten there yet. I wish I could say I've accepted change just like I've accepted growing pains; it's going to hurt but at least I'll get taller. But, I'm working on it.

I still love my home of St. Joseph, all the people that have brought me closer to Christ throughout my middle and high school years, and I still love the youth center that fostered so many great conversations and memories, even if it looks different physically. I will leave St. Joseph in a few months, but I will return despite the change, because one thing will always remain: the love we have for each other and the love we have for our Lord.

5. Writing: Embarrassment and Growth

I wrote my first story in first-grade. I had co-authored some other stories with friends, but this one was my first solo endeavor. I began writing on thick lined white paper—the kind you use to practice the alphabet when you're just learning. We were learning grammar and spelling, so I decided to put my new knowledge to the test and try writing a book worthy of the Pulitzer Prize. The idea came to me during class one day, right before free-time. I needed something to do so I decided on writing a story like the one my classmates and I wrote. We would each take turns writing a chapter and it was *always* about animals. The most recent story we had worked on was about mother and daughter horses that were fighting an evil enemy. I knew I had to write about animals, so I decided on a noble cat queen who had her beloved crown stolen by a mysterious civilian.

The plot was truly original and exhilarating. The story focuses on a queen of an unknown country (who happens to be a cat), whose crown is stolen right off her head. She makes the long journey to find a psychic cat named Felix (spelled Felicks in the original copy) who can see who has her crown. The story continues in a sloppy and barely readable fashion. The major plot points escape me, but I know eventually, she figured out that she had been fooled by the psychic and he was really the one who stole her beloved crown.

The cat queen story ended there, after the Queen retrieved her crown from the sleazy psychic. I wrote one more work that year titled "Brown Beauty" As suggested by the title, it was inspired by the classic *Black Beauty*. My friend accused me of copying the idea, but I was adamant that my creation was completely original; this horse was brown, *not* black. However, no copyright claim ever came my way. "Brown Beauty" remains incomplete and sits somewhere in my room stapled at the corner and curling at the ends, stiff with age, the cat queen story on top of it. That was my final creative work that year. Instead of using those thick lined papers to write thrilling novels, I used them to improve my handwriting so one day someone could actually read my stories instead of trying to interpret the scribble.

Although that was the last of my endeavors in my first-grade class, my love for literature carried on throughout elementary school. I looked forward to the days when my class would go to the library, so I could check out the maximum number of books possible. The library is an average size but felt huge to a petite girl like me. I felt like Belle in *The Beauty and the Beast*, climbing the ladder to reach the books on the top shelf, taking in the magnificence of all the literature.

The library was split into a few different sections. In the middle was the librarian's desk and a small classroom setting where we would do the assignment for that day. To the left of the desk was the fiction section. A few bookcases with novels of all varieties stacked together were up against the wall. I would often peruse through this section picking out the books I thought looked interesting. I had criteria of what I identified as a "good book." The cover had to have bright colors and a pretty font. If the book was narrated by a boy I would put it down. The book had to be relatively short; I wouldn't pick anything up that was more than 300 pages. Big books were daunting, and I didn't have a lick of patience. There was a short period of time in fourth or fifth grade when my classmates were trying to tackle *Hugo Cabret*. The book looked monstrous, and I couldn't fathom sitting down to read all those words. I had a hard time sitting down to read even modestly sized novels. I remember checking out multiple books at a time just because I knew that two or three would lose my interest in the first thirty pages. (I was a tough critic as a child, mostly because my hyperactive brain could not calm down to read a good book.)

The second section, which was also to the left of the librarian desk, but towards the back of the room was where the "little kid" books were. The bookshelves were only two feet off the ground and formed a U shape around a small area with carpet squares and stools. My early elementary years were spent here. When we went to the library we always had an assignment to do which I would rush to get done so I could grab the best seat in the little nook and pull out a bunch of books from the shelves to read. Eventually this space bored me along with the books, which were no thicker than my pinky finger. I graduated to the other fiction section once we were allowed to do so.

The last section took up the entire right side of the library: the nonfiction section. I spent the least time here, only looking through the tall shelves when I had a project that needed research. There aren't exactly memoirs geared towards children under the age of eleven. If there were, I would have been all over them.

Sometimes, if I already had a good reading pile, I would help the librarian put away books, something that made me feel like an adult. There was always a cart full of books that she hadn't yet put back in their place. If I walked in and it was full, I knew that I had a job once I finished my work. Again, I rushed to finish my assignment—if there were already too many girls helping put away books I would be told to sit down. When I first started helping out, she only allowed me to put away the "little kid" books, although I disobeyed and grabbed a whole stack of all genres to put in their place.

When the school library books weren't enough, my Mom would take me to the public library and I'd pick out novels for "older kids," hoping that my mom wouldn't make me put them back on the shelf before we got to the checkout line. Wendy Mass novels were popular among my friends. We would read them all at the same time, if there were enough copies in the library. *Every Soul a Star* and *A Mango-Shaped Space* were our favorites. We also loved all the books Mass wrote about birthdays: *11 Birthdays, 12 Finally,* and *13 Gifts.* I would devour these books, each one making me want to be one year older. Many times, they would stack up in the back of my desk until the next time my teacher would take us in a single file line to the library.

My love for literature continued into middle school, and really hit me like a strong wind in my seventh-grade language arts class. I had Mrs. Heer, a sweet mother of three who was also the director of the musical at my middle school. We read Jack London's *Call of the Wild* and *Watership Down*. I still visited the school's library quite often. I would go in the mornings and pick out books to read during the school day. (I got in trouble for reading during class a few times.)

In middle school I had my first real encounter with poetry other than acrostics we wrote to describe ourselves at the beginning of every school year. One day, Mrs. Heer went around the room handing out copies of "The Negro Speaks of Rivers" by Langston Hughes, telling us that we would be analyzing it as a class. I didn't know how to mark up a poem or what to look for, but Langston Hughes made it easy. His language flowed through the poem effortlessly, creating meaning and beauty at the same time. His writing not only shows us something but takes us somewhere: "I've known rivers ancient as the world and older than the/ flow of human blood in human veins" says Hughes at the beginning of the poem. His words create a heightened sense of reality with increasing drama in so few words. Langston Hughes's poetry was like a firm handshake welcoming me into the world of literature.

We unpacked all the language and devices of the poem in class. We connected the context of the poem to the references

Hughes makes to different rivers in the continent of Africa. Mrs. Heer dropped hints as to why Hughes wrote what he wrote, encouraging us to realize his message for ourselves. When we got to the line "I've seen its muddy/ bosom turn all golden in the sunset," we sat for a moment pondering what it could mean. One student raised his hand, asking the teacher, "Uh, what is a boss-um?"

The whole class erupted in giggles, including Mrs. Heer. Our serious analysis of a legendary poem was interrupted by silly middle-school humor.

"Does anyone want to explain what a *bosom* is?" said Mrs. Heer, correcting the student's pronunciation while suppressing her own amusement. Other students hesitantly raised their hands and danced around the real meaning of the word until finally the teacher put an end to the boy's confusion.

Although immature humor interrupted our deep discussion of Hughes's commentary on race and heritage, it still stuck in the back of my brain, his words shaping and molding my mind towards a path filled with rich language.

In the fall of my eighth-grade year, I visited the open house of a magnet arts high school in Towson, Maryland. I visited with the intention of learning more about their cosmetology program. I spent my middle school afternoons watching online hair tutorials and nail art videos and was convinced it was the career path for me. My mom disagreed and thought that I should do something "more practical." I walked into the cosmetology classroom to see a line of girls my age stretching to the back of the room, and about fifty mannequin heads lining the tops of shelves, eyes not blinking. I reached the end of the line and stood in it with my Mom, who was clearly unimpressed. It was like a hundred eyes were on me, the mannequins and the other girls waiting to schedule a shadow day. It didn't feel right. I was utterly disappointed; looking forward to an event for weeks only to find it underwhelming can be discouraging. I looked at my mom with defeated eyes that said, "You were right," and we walked out of the room, leaving the freaky heads behind me.

My heart was still focused on the arts school, even though my aspirations for being a cosmetologist were over. My mom took me to the Literary Arts presentation, knowing my love for reading. I was ready to go home, but I remained behind my mom, walking up the steps, and trying to navigate the school.

The room was crowded with prospective students and their parents who were probably more concerned with the school than they were. There was an air of comfort and quirkiness to the room. Large bean bags were at the front of the classroom (something I had never seen inside a school before) and the wall was scattered with posters of quotes from famous writers and books. The teacher described the program and the freshman students talked about how much they loved the class. They spoke about analyzing poetry and writing workshops, guest teachers and writing competitions. It was a wonderland of literature and it was pulling me in each second. I wanted to audition right then and there. I couldn't wait until January in case I somehow lost all my writing skill in a few months. I walked out of the room ready to go home and read every book I was going to read over the summer. Most importantly, my mom liked the program, another feat that I never thought we would overcome.

"It sounds like you, Lauren," said my mom as we left the school crowded with hundreds of students.

Months later, in February, I got a letter containing my scores on the entrance exams for all the magnet schools I applied for. I eagerly tore open the envelope at my dining room table. I didn't expect much from Carver Center, the arts school that I visited in October. I had gotten into another magnet school closer to me, and I even passed the exam for Carver, however because of the competitiveness of the program I was waitlisted at number five. Again, I didn't expect to go. *There was no way five people would drop out of a program like this,* I thought. But in late March, when my mom was driving me home from band practice, she said she had some news.

"The school called me today," said my mother. My mind went immediately to my middle school and I searched my thoughts wondering what I could've done in the past week to cause the school to call my mom. I was terrified of getting in trouble, especially with my mother.

"Oh gosh, what did I do?" I responded, trying to make a joke about it in case I actually did do something. (Avoiding uncomfortable situations with humor was something I did all the time.)

"No, Carver called me." I looked at my mom, raising my eyebrows to see if I was right about what she was suggesting.

"They offered you a spot in Literary Arts."

"Really?" My Mom nodded, and I swelled with happiness and relief, but mostly shock. I reached for my phone, ready to call my friends who had also got in to tell them that the last of us had been accepted. When we got home, I ran to the home phone as fast as I could, dropping my school bags on the floor. I needed to hear the message for myself.

Before encountering the creative writing program, I thought I had reached the peak of my relationship with literature. The only thing left to do was keep on reading. Seeing a whole program dedicated to the craft deepened and expanded the little box that I had put writing in. Without it, I would have neglected my love of writing altogether, simply because I wouldn't have had anyone telling me that writing was worthwhile and important after middle school. If I had lived in another county, or simply went to the school I was zoned for, I wouldn't have had the opportunities in writing that I've had these past four years. There doesn't seem to be any room for creative writing in school lessons anymore. It pains me to think that a young writer like myself loses their passion for writing just because it was not encouraged at the school they attended.

I went back to school that Monday with a newfound confidence in my writing. I had been accepted into a fancy arts school that only a few other people from my school had gotten into. This confidence translated into a new writing project for our eighth-grade language arts class. We had just finished reading *A Tale of Two Cities* by Charles Dickens. Ms. Johnson, our teacher, who had the energy equivalent of a squirrel on roller skates, had assigned us a poetry project that showcased Dickens's use of light and darkness. I was ready to take on the challenge. By this time, I had told all my classmates I made it into the competitive writing program at an arts school, so I knew they were expecting the best from me. After she gave us the assignment my shoulders perked up, and I eyed the rest of the classroom. Most had scowls and were quietly groaning at having to imitate a writer as complex and longwinded as Dickens. But I held a wide smile, knowing that *I* was qualified to write this poem. After all, I had written a poem that got me into Carver.

I sat on my bed that night with my laptop open, typing and re-typing until I had the perfect concoction of emotion and technique. My fingers moved faster with every idea that came to my head. I wrote with vigor, my words fueling my brain to the next stanza. I wrote the whole poem the night it was assigned so I didn't waste any precious idea that came to my brain during the school day. At the time, I thought my idea was original and creative. I was ready to share my masterpiece with my classmates when we had to peer edit each other's poems.

I paired up with a few of my friends and we read each other's poems, proofreading it as we went. When I got mine back from my friend, there were no marks on it.

"I thought it was perfect," she said. I smiled a knowing smirk and said thank you while proceeding to tell her what I found that was wrong with her poem. "Mine is so bad," she complained. "I wish mine was like yours."

"All you have to do is edit! Trust me, it's not that bad," I responded, trying to comfort her. She sighed and smiled at me, as if to thank me for helping her. In a few days, we had to present our poem in front of the class. The teacher taught us projection and eye contact the next class and then sent us home to practice. I stood in front of my mirror in my room, and, making sure the door was closed, I repeated my poem until I felt that I delivered the message properly. I went to school the next day, paper in hand and waited my turn anxiously during class to read my poem, determined to move middle schoolers with my words. After poems read with monotony and little drama, it came time for my friend whose poem I edited to present her poem. I hadn't read her revised poem, so I was excited to see what she had come up with and if she took my suggestions. It made me feel like an English teacher, with her as my first student.

As she was reading her poem, I noticed a familiar theme. When it came to the end of her poem, I read mine over once more, picking out some lines that she had copied verbatim. I glanced over at another classmate who had read my poem, widening my eyes to silently tell her "That's practically *my* poem she read." I was beyond upset. I kept tapping my foot, itching to get up to the podium where everybody read their poems. I knew my poem was better since she was the one who copied me, but would everyone else know that? What about the teacher? It didn't feel right that she presented before me, and now it would seem like I was the cheater. To make it better, only one person was to perform in between us. When it finally became my turn to present the poem, I read the poem aloud but was shaken by the previous events. I read the poem with just as much monotony as the students who couldn't care less about poetry. I sat down disappointed in myself and my friend. My disappointment rose when I got my poem back graded with a large "C" written at the top. I was insulted. How could my language arts teacher not recognize good poetry when she saw it? I ended up keeping quiet about my copycat and my undeserving grade, and the year passed with little opportunity to redeem myself.

If you were to ask me now, my language arts teacher in eighth-grade was being nice for giving me a C. The poem was so atrocious I can't even read it without physically curling in on myself. I read it once for my literary classmates in my sophomore year, and I couldn't get through the first stanza without laugh-cringing.

After that fiasco in middle school, I'd like to think that my writing has improved (and my ego has decreased) since that time. The one thing that hasn't changed is my gravitation towards poetry. With poetry, there is no limits, With the right techniques and literary devices, a good poem can be about absolutely anything and still be beautiful. Like Langston Hughes, who writes about his African ancestry in the midst of racism and discrimination. Despite the ugliness that surrounds him, it is his soul that reigns in the poem.

With the words of Langston Hughes stuck to my brain and many books (good and bad) floating in my memory, I finally entered the literary arts program at my new high school.

Throughout my time in the program, so many words have been written, re-written, read, and analyzed. It has been almost five years since I read that Langston Hughes poem that launched me into a never-ending sphere of wordplay. Literature goes so deep that even if one memorized all of the greatest authors and their works, they wouldn't even scratch the surface of what is out there. And certainly, I have not either.

There is so much I don't know about literature even though it was my focus for four years and probably four more. Although one can't know everything there is to know about literature, the growth that every writer achieves is definitely worthwhile. Writing every day gives me an excuse to empty all the mess that is in my mind. (When you're a teenager, there's a lot.) My ideas have changed and morphed into completely different ones. I've put emotions on the page with the angst of a thousand teenagers and have kept a professional voice in articles where I felt like screaming. When you write, you get to know yourself a little too well. Through writing, I create a deep relationship with my innermost thoughts. My soul woven through every piece. My soul growing deep like rivers.

6. My Beverage of Choice

There is one thing I know as a fact, and it is that lemonade is by far the best beverage. I've never heard of anyone disliking lemonade. It may not be everybody's favorite, but it's never anybody's least favorite. People have a hatred for Coke or Pepsi, cranberry juice or milk, but no one finds anything hateful about lemonade. How could you? It is the summer beverage of picnics and neighborhood block parties. Even the look of it is cheerful, a tall glass of a pastel yellow lemonade mingling with ice cubes just begs refreshment. It is the business for enthusiastic children trying to make a dollar off friendly dog-walkers—it is the 25-cent token for a good deed. Fresh-squeezed, homemade lemonade is like arts and crafts in the kitchen, a mess over the counter ending in sticky hands and a pitcher of sunshine.

Lemonade is like my neighborhood. Bright, cheery, and refreshing. It is something to look forward to, seeing all the kids and neighbors outside on a bright day. My neighborhood is full of families with kids young and old, enrolled in kindergarten to graduated from college. Our neighborhood is named "Glenside Farms," as said on a sign at the end of a long private drive. The place where we live now used to be a huge farm. Fields of crops and livestock scattered across the little corner of Perry Hall. Now houses and pavement replace what I assumed was a large expanse of green lawn, with only the street names to remember them. I live on a street called "Hayloft" and the road adjacent to us is "Dorothy Fields." The street names put together some kind of landscape in our minds, helping us imagine what was once bull-dozed. The only remnants of a farm are the goats on the drive into the neighborhood. The road, named Gerst, holds a small house with tractors scattered about the lawn. Also on the lawn but to the side is a fence holding in a bunch of ornery goats. The fence fails more times than it succeeds, and the goats are free to wander on the road, disrupting the little traffic that travels through it. The goats are the most headstrong animals in the world; they will look straight at the headlights of your car and plant their hooves, not moving as if saying, "Go ahead, I bet you won't." Many times, my family has been trapped by the stubborn goats in the road, strolling across the asphalt like it's a crosswalk. Remarkably, none of them have been hit yet. Most people don't complain and only laugh at the goat's lack of consideration for drivers. My mom loves them, seeing them running free reminds her of Ireland, her own Mother's homeland.

Most of my neighbors are nicer and more considerate than the goats on the road. They are kind, compassionate, and caring people. My family moved there when I was two, when my Mom was about to give birth to my younger sister. My mom and I were walking around the neighborhood one day, getting to know the area, when a young boy who lived down the street called over to us. He was a year older than me and asked if I wanted to eat taco-cheese with him on the porch. It is the only memory I have of meeting someone in the neighborhood. My two-year old brain probably couldn't hold that much information, and I guess it decided my taco-cheese friend was the most important.

After that all my neighbors were just there. I was too young to remember the "getting to know you" stage of moving and meeting people. All of a sudden, the parents were out on the street talking about the goings-on in Glenside, while the children rode bikes in circles until someone fell. My sister and I would go outside onto the burning hot pavement and humid Maryland heat, and play until someone saw us through the window and dragged their parents outside to join us. That's what the summer would look like.

It was then when someone would have cans of lemonade (or a different carbonated beverage, but lemonade was the best, obviously) in their refrigerator and offer them to the kids playing. We'd drop whatever we were doing and go take our drink and sit on the curb. We'd laugh about something nonsensical or be forced to play duck-duck-goose by the youngest child. Then we'd put our cans on the pavement and rush back to riding bikes or playing "house" or games of softball in someone's back yard until the parents told us to clean up our mess.

I am a few years older than most of the children in my neighborhood, which provided many babysitting jobs, but also added so much to my growing up. Not only did I have my one younger sister, Olivia, whom I love dearly, I had many who would knock on my door after school, asking us to play. I grew close with many of them and felt responsible to always behave and act right—I owed it to them to show them the right way. I know I failed sometimes because I'm growing too, but having those kids run through my yard yelling "Lauren! Olivia! Come play!" made me a better person.

During the school year it got darker earlier, and our little get togethers were cut short because of the early darkness. But a new tradition would pick up in September, when the bus would drop us all off after elementary school. My neighbor across the street, Kara, and her older brother, Kevin, played football after school every day, and since it was hard to play with two people, they would ask me to join.

I didn't know anything about football and although I understand it now, I still don't understand what we did when we played their rendition of it. After the bus dropped us off, I'd drop my book bag by the tree on their lawn and wait until they told me what to do. We played across their driveway using the two trees on either side as end zones. I ran where they told me to run and tried to catch the ball when they threw it to me. Though I could never hold onto it, and more often than not I would end up face first on the driveway, the ball two feet in front of me with a skinned knee instead of a touchdown. Kevin was always the permanent quarterback, and he would throw to me or Kara (his best bet was Kara) whenever there was an opening, which was always since his only defender was a barely four-foot girl with wrists the circumference of a twig. I remember feeling stressed, hoping that if I closed my eyes and prayed that the ball would land just the right way in my arms, so I could slide into the mulch around the tree.

That fantasy disappeared when Kevin's friends would come over to play after school. They were older, taller, scarier, and meaner than I was, and of all sports to play with them, it had to be football. One of his friends who came over often was a big Italian kid whose mom owned a pizza place and drove a convertible. I knew when he stayed on the bus past his stop that he was coming to play with us and the rest of the ride would fill me with dread. I was always worried that he wouldn't abide by the "two hand touch" type of ball we played and would push me down with his boy hands. I wouldn't stand a chance. He and Kevin would hop off the bus after Kara and me (big kids always sat in the back) and the only thing I could do was keep on walking toward their house, knowing I couldn't bow out or use homework as an excuse, because what kind of third grader has homework?

"You can't even kick a football!" Kevin's friend yelled during one of our football games, laughing at my pathetic play.

"You don't know that," I responded casually, pretending I didn't care. Whenever I complained about girls at school, my mom would always tell me that I can't let people like that get to me. And I wasn't about to let him walk all over me, just because he looked scary and could eat me in three bites.

"Fine. Show me then." He leaned to the side and laughed, looking at Kevin as if to say, "This is gonna be good." I took on the challenge and placed the football on the little stand they had placed on the asphalt. I stepped back, preparing myself for the kick, trying to emulate the kickers I saw on Sunday night games. In one swift move, I stepped forward with my left foot and swung my right towards the ball. I missed wildly, my foot inches away from the ball, and nothing but the wind blowing by to send it toppling over pathetically on the pavement, rolling towards the street.

"See!" my challenger responded, throwing his arms out in front of him, gesturing to my failed attempt to prove him wrong.

"Whatever. At least I can throw one," I said, trying to salvage any dignity the football had taken away from me. But I was still embarrassed I couldn't prove to the older kids that I could in fact kick a football. So, I went home, and like a drunkard with his beer, I drowned my sorrows in a glass of lemonade.

The lemonade season extended into the last weeks of the summer; school would be in full swing, and it would still be poured into glasses of ice. But after September ended, the weather switched and so did our beverage of choice. Lemonade was switched to jugs of apple cider bought at the local farmer's market or orchard. Apple cider is the real drink of fall, not any of that pumpkin spice nonsense. Although it isn't as good as lemonade, apple cider still embodies everything that fall is. You can drink it hot on the chilly days and over ice on the warm ones, with your friends over a campfire, or by yourself with a blanket and a book to keep you company. Fall didn't begin until we cracked open a jug of apple cider.

We'd normally stock up on apple cider when we went

apple picking. I loved apple picking; if I could do it year-round, I would. My family never went when I was little. It was only when my friend invited me in middle school, that I went for the first time. My mom, sister, and I went up to the orchard after getting lost a few times on the windy back roads, but eventually we made it. After meeting up with our friends we were given wicker baskets to pile all our apples in. I felt like a little farm girl from the 1800s, getting fruit the old-fashioned way before they were bought in grocery stores. My friend, Josie, and I (who was actually allergic to apples) scoured the whole orchard looking at the different types of apples: Gala, Fuji, McIntosh, Golden Delicious, Empire, Granny Smith, and more. We tried to find the tiny ones to take home and put on our desks. Josie's mom followed around with a peeler, so we could eat apples as we picked. After our skinny arms couldn't haul around overflowing baskets of apples, we went to the top of the hill waiting for the truck to take us back to the main part of the farm. They weighed our apples and put them in big brown paper bags. I was disappointed we couldn't keep the wicker baskets. But, I got over it quickly because we were heading to the store, which sold pre-picked apples, homemade apple cider, and those glorious apple cider donuts. Josie accompanied me while I walked around drinking the samples of apple cider. We wandered around the store pretending to be interested in every display of farm-fresh food just so our moms wouldn't tell us it was time to go home and separate. Eventually the call from our mothers came, and Josie and I sauntered out of the little store to the gravel parking lot where the moms and sisters stood waiting.

"Why don't you ride together?" said Josie's mom, gesturing to Josie, our sisters, and me. I looked at Josie and nodded my head quickly.

"Yeah! It would be fun!" I said, pulling Josie's arm toward my mom's car and hopping in, so quick she couldn't say no yet.

We sat in the car the hour drive back, listening to music and devouring the apple cider donuts that we bought inside the store. My mom only bought a half a dozen, and by the time we arrived home there were only two left. Each of us had one while in the car, except for me, who had two, and Josie, who had none (I justified my two by saying I ate one for Josie.) It was when we reached her house that we departed, our hands sticky from apple picking and donut eating. We said goodbye to Josie and her sister, walking away yelling from our car that we must do it again.

Apple picking became a yearly event after that day at the orchard with Josie. We would go every year, either as a family or with friends, to pick apples at a different local orchard. One time we went too late in the season and the apple orchard had run out of apples, so we had to pick seconds off the ground. It wasn't the same feeling as the first time we went. I didn't feel like a little farm girl when I went and picked a seemingly perfect apple off the ground just to find it rotten on the other side. Another year we went with a neighbor family to a place called Paulus orchard. The place wasn't as exciting as the first one. There weren't as many types of apples, but there was a play area and three little girls with a ton of energy, which added plenty of excitement as is.

After making the trip up, we tried picking apples, but the girls eventually lost interest and turned their attention to the big play area with a slide, corn maze, a big spider web net to jump on. Kenleigh, the youngest, went running from attraction to attraction, never staying on one thing for more than five minutes. She reminded me of how I was as a toddler, or at least what my mother told me I was like. I had an attention span shorter than a goldfish, and couldn't stay focused on one activity, no matter how much I liked it. My mom would get a toy out for me to play with and by the time she had set it all up I had already moved onto something new. That's how Kenleigh was, too. We spent a while running around, following her from one thing to the next. I finally knew how my mom felt when she had to deal with me. (She still has to deal with me, but I'm slightly more manageable now, I hope.) We spent the day running around the Paulus Playland as it was called, acting like our toddler selves, letting our short attention spans take over for one day.

Like all toddlers, we eventually got hungry, and both our families walked down to the little stand that sold food at the orchard. I can't remember what I got for lunch, but the one thing I do remember were the warm, sugary, and soft apple cider donuts I ate for dessert. I ordered one with my meal; it's obligatory at an apple orchard to have their own rendition of the apple cider donut, especially if you're a donut connoisseur like myself. I bit into it while it was still warm—the best time to eat an apple cider donut. The warm cake collapsed in my mouth, releasing a wave of autumnal flavors over my tongue; just enough apple, just enough sugar, and perfectly warm so the moisture of the donut remains in your mouth as you eat. It was a masterpiece.

"How's the donut?" my dad asked, knowing my acquired taste for the dessert.

"Amazing," I said, muffled through the donut still in my mouth. He chuckled at my love for the donut over everything else, but eventually understood when he had a taste for himself. I now understood why the apple orchard was just mediocre. They had used all their good apples to make the apple cider donuts! It makes for an average orchard, but an amazing donut and I wasn't complaining. I convinced my parents (and my neighbors) to get a dozen of the apple cider donuts that I now claimed to be the best I've ever had.

There was a line just for a fresh dozen of donuts. My mom and I hopped into the line right away. It was long, and I was extra antsy, knowing that donuts were so close.

After the longest ten or so minutes ever, the two dozen donuts were in my hand, all warm and sugary having just been fried and rolled in the sweet seasoning. I brought them over to the little picnic tables outside of the country store, and in my loud announcer voice, brought the good news to the people. "Donuts are here!" I proclaimed, and I ate another one, and probably another one too. I can't remember, but if I did, I know they were just as good the second and third time around.

We sat under the little pavilion at the picnic table. It was raining, but it still felt warm. Warm from the donuts, warm from the fall sweaters my mom made us bring from home, and warm from all the little hugs and laughter from my neighbors. When the rain finally died down we carried that warmth to our golden Honda minivan, and drove all the way home, with our neighbors following behind us. We pulled up at the same time, our driveways right next to each other. The girls climbed out of their SUV and ran toward us like they hadn't seen us in years, greeting us with smiles, and running with their arms open.

Sometimes, when I come home from school or sports practice, I arrive the same time as my little neighbors. This is often the only time I see them anymore. Our short attention spans drove us to busy lifestyles in separate directions. They are still a young family with many after-school games to play, apple orchards to visit, and years of school to attend. I wish I could see them more often: the little girls who became my family for the earlier years of my life. But that warmth felt under the pavilion on the rainy fall day at Paulus orchard comes flooding back whenever Kenleigh yells "Lauren!" from across our conjoined lawn. Or when I watch Sunday football games with my Dad, reminding me of my three-man team across the street. That warmth comes back in small spontaneous smiles in the middle of the day, when I read a book, or see some little kid that reminds me of those lemonade and apple-cider moments. I feel that warmth in glasses and glasses of overly sweet lemonade, apple cider, and heaping handfuls of taco-cheese.

7. Camping Memoir #2

My grandfather sold the trailer about four or five years into my sister and I going to camp. We knew camp would continue, but without the trailer, it would be different. Traditions would have to change, and the symbolism of that place would soon disappear into the hands of someone who was not us. I asked my dad countless times if he could buy it from my grandfather, so we could still go there. He said no.

I had a bad habit from crying every time I left somewhere I knew I wasn't going back to for a while. I cried when we left our grandparents house in Johnstown—we only went there for Thanksgiving and Easter. I cried when we left Rehoboth beach—that was only once a year. And man, did I bawl when we left Disney world—that was only twice in my lifetime so far. I remember being teary-eyed when we left camp, but I wasn't crying. The sentimentality of the place wasn't the caliber of the other girls who had been going there every year for almost ten years by that time.

My family was usually the last to leave camp every year, since it was our grandparents who owned the place. I always hated being the last ones to leave, because with everybody gone it wasn't camp weekend anymore, even though we were still there. It was just a trailer in the middle of nowhere, surrounded by the sounds of tree leaves hitting against each other in the wind, rather than the loud yells and music blasting from a car stereo.

I watched my friend Emma and her family pull up the gravel entryway to the camp, and almost to the road when the car stopped, and started reversing back down the hill, the gravel making a continuous crunch beneath the wheels. When they were almost at the base, Emma hopped out, her face wet with tears, and grabbed a rock from the ground: something to remember camp by. She got back in the car, and they drove back up and onto the road, leaving us the last ones at camp.

When we finally packed up my uncle's car, full of camp gear, leftover food, and us, we drove up the hill to the road, the gravel making that crunching sound below the wheels that used to fill me with excitement for the arrival at camp. I made sure that I looked hard at the trailer and the woods surrounding it, telling my future self not to forget what it looked like. I looked until we were too far away from the road, and the thick coverage of trees obscured my view of the old place that would pass onto someone else. The trailer was soon torn down by the new owners, probably for good reasons; it was old and had run its course, petered out from holding a bunch of young girls for years. I asked my dad the next year if we could ask the new owners to go back for camp weekend. He said no, that it wouldn't be right. But I didn't care, since I didn't let go of that place until the "future self" my younger one was yelling at really did forget what the trailer looked like.

8. Overcrowded

In middle school, I would sit at a lunch table so crowded I could barely fit my butt on the bench. It was the table right in front of the entrance to the lunchroom. My friends and I decided on the first bus ride to school that this was where we would meet to avoid being the token lonely kid who always sits alone like we saw in the movies. We never moved from that table, not once in the whole three years I was there. And never once was it not crowded. I sat shoulder to shoulder, squeezed in between two girls while we ate our packed lunches. Even on that first day of school, kids kept piling into the lunchroom, asking to sit down next to us—I guess we had friendly faces—and although there wasn't enough elbow room to go around, we couldn't say no.

Our middle school was overcrowded. There were about 500 kids in my grade alone, and over 1,500 in the whole school. My only understanding of middle school came from movies or TV shows. I thought being so short and tiny, all the eighth graders would tower over me, and large stampedes of hungry prepubescent children would run me over on the way to lunch. Even though what I thought I knew turned out to be less dramatic, spending three years of my life in a place where popularity was the most coveted status proved to be difficult. (As it is for every student.)

After living through three different schools at three different ages, I know now that middle school is the worst by far. Elementary school kids are cute with their overbearing energy and their smiles with missing teeth, but once they enter sixth grade, everything goes south. Being in middle school is the smelliest experience. Nobody knows what deodorant is yet, and gym class is required every single year, resulting in a whole lot of stink, and in a school as big as mine, it multiplies and spreads. Not only that, the idea of popularity is still something students think is a key to success. I once had a friend tell me in sixth grade that she had to be popular in middle school because she wanted practice for being an actress when she was older. It sounded silly then and now I just roll my eyes.

Being popular didn't appeal to me, so I focused on being just the opposite. My friends and I would sneer and turn up our noses at the so-called "popular kids," feeling that we were too mature for such petty recognition. We prided ourselves on not wasting our time trying to impress others. Little did we know, our attitude made us just as immature as the ones we criticized. But that's how everyone was. Middle school can be described as a pile of dirty socks waiting to be washed on the floor of your bedroom: they stink, they're missing a match, and they just keep piling up.

I was once in this dirty pile of socks as everyone once was. Some may argue I still am. High school is equally messy, but in a different way—think a whole hamper of dirty clothing, but this time your Mom won't wash it for you. But in middle school, everyone is equally confused but won't admit it. It's that weird in between stage of being awake and falling asleep.

The first sock in my pile came during the summer leading up to sixth grade. It was June, probably eighty degrees at this point but I can't be sure; Maryland weather tends to throw curve balls every other week. Jessica, my best friend, and I were in the front yard along with the rest of the neighborhood. She lived only a few houses behind me—if I walked to the end of my street and looked around the corner, I could see her house right there facing the road. I had known Jessica since I was two years old. Our mothers met in the local park. She was one of those friends I don't remember meeting. She was always just there in my memory, having play dates together every day until we were too old to call them that anymore.

Jessica and I were just about to walk to my backyard before she stopped and turned around. She stood right in front of the small three-foot tree next to the garage, her foot an inch away from where the path to the back patio began. I was in front of her, still on the driveway, and confused, wondering why she stopped.

"I'm moving," she said. She didn't introduce it lightly, or sit me down saying, "I have something I need to tell you" with her hand sympathetically on my shoulder. She just told me. And then she laughed. "I don't know why I'm laughing," she said in between her fits of giggling, "Every time I've told someone, I just break out laughing." I guess this was her own way of coping, avoiding the uncomfortable situation.

"What do you mean? Are you joking?" I said, hoping that her laughter meant she was playing a prank on me. Jessica wasn't the most trustworthy person; she would often make up stories and tall tales about things she'd done or seen, but all kids made up stuff at that age and if they didn't they were foolish enough to believe them, like me. One time she tried to convince me to sneak out of my house in the middle of the night to meet at the park where we always hung out. I told her no, since I couldn't sneak out without my parents knowing. But she still persisted, until I agreed that I would at least *try* to meet her in the middle of the night. Of course, I stayed in my bed the entire night, not taking a step towards the door. The next day she told me she was waiting for me by herself at the park and I never showed. I said sorry, and took her word for it, but I wasn't that foolish, and after her asking me to sneak out a few more times I knew there was no way she was telling the truth.

We sat on the little stone ledge surrounding the three-foot tree in my mom's garden and she explained to me that her dad got promoted so they had to move to Florida for his job. I believed her, like all the times before, but this time, I didn't *want* to believe her. All the future memories we would have together dissipated into the muggy Maryland heat that morning. Suddenly, everything felt hot, the air hugging me tightly as if to keep me from breathing.

"Are you coming back?" I asked.

"I don't know. Probably not," she responded, shrugging

her shoulders as if it was a perfectly casual conversation. Then we both got up and continued on the little stone path to my backyard. We said nothing else about the matter.

Jessica and I had another friend named Claire. She lived behind Jessica, who lived behind me. We were all in a line, each within walking distance of each other. I met Claire through Jessica in elementary school and we would often meet at the park in my neighborhood to play Mulchman—a game where one person would close her eyes and try to touch someone else, or try to yell "Mulchman" while somebody was walking on the mulch; if you were caught you became the Mulchman. We always played this after school, even if it was only three of us.

A few weeks after Jessica had told me the news, we met at the playground as usual. Claire already knew that Jessica would be leaving for Florida soon, and we all played Mulchman, ignoring the fact that by the end of the summer, there would only be two of us, making the game obsolete. None of us had cried yet, or at least we didn't tell each other about it. Jessica wasn't emotional, but I was. To put it in sixth grader terms, she was cool. She wasn't a baby. She never once faltered in her stoic nature, and never let me in on what she was feeling. I remember her saying kids' television shows were stupid. The only one we ever watched together was a kid version of *Survivor*. Even though Jessica wasn't the sentimental type, I was always emotional and would cry at the slightest change in the atmosphere. Jessica, on the other hand, would make the atmosphere change to her liking. If we were playing a game and I was winning, she would change it. That's just how she was, no tears and no worry; if she was there, she was in control.

Moving to Florida was the one time Jessica wasn't in control. She couldn't pick Florida up and move it right next to Maryland, or even say at the last minute that this was a summer long test to see if Claire and I would actually be sad if she had to move. She couldn't change the game even if she wanted to. It was one of the last times we hung out before she would leave at the end of the summer for Florida. So, after our final game of Mulchman, Jessica sat on the black plastic ridge surrounding the playground. Claire sat next to her and then I joined. All three of us were crouched down squatting on the small plastic ridge not meant for sitting. Then we cried. Not just Claire and I, but all of us, Jessica too. We held each other and cried over all the things that we would miss together in middle school and then high school like we'd planned. On the little black plastic ridge only about four inches thick, we cried together for the first and last time.

After that, they walked me home. And then Jessica moved to Florida.

A few weeks later, after middle school had begun and anxiety about new friends replaced my anxiety about not seeing my old friend, I got a call from Claire. We became close friends after Jessica had moved, and we played Mulchman with other neighborhood girls on afternoons.

"Jessica's on the phone. I'm gonna let you talk to her," said Claire, when I picked up the home phone.

"Really?" I said. I hadn't heard from Jessica in weeks and Claire and I rarely ever talked about her.

"Yeah, I have two phones, I'm gonna put them next to each other so you two can talk." I scrunched up my eyebrows. I didn't understand why Jessica couldn't just ask Claire for my home phone if she forgot it. The fact that Jessica forgot my phone number was surprising itself. She called me countless times all throughout elementary school asking if I could come over. I had Jessica's former home phone number fresh in my memory. If I ever called and she wasn't there, her young, squeaky voice came over the robotic speaker, reminding me of her phone number at the end of every voice mail. Now she called Claire, asked her to call me on a separate phone, then put the two phones close to each other so we could speak. It seemed like so much work. Nevertheless, Claire put the phones next to each other, so Jessica and I could finally speak. I imagine her holding the two phones together, sitting on her living room couch, listening closely and trying to be quiet so we wouldn't hear her eavesdropping.

"Hey!" I said, excited to finally speak with my friend since summer. "I've missed you a lot."

"Yeah, me too!" Jessica responded.

"What's your new phone number, so I can call you more often. We haven't spoken in weeks."

"Oh, I haven't memorized it yet. I'll let you know, though," said Jessica, hesitating before she answered my question. We continued to talk for about two more minutes. It was too short.

"You guys done yet?" Claire blurted into the two receivers.

"Yeah, we're good," I responded. Jessica and I said our goodbyes, and then Claire hung up the phones.

That was the last time I ever spoke to Jessica on the phone. I found out later that Jessica did know what her home phone was and just didn't want to give it to me. I was texting Claire later that year (we finally got cell phones, the ones that slid up to reveal the keyboard were a hot commodity) when she told me she was with Jessica, who was visiting from Florida, but failed to let me know. I communicated through Claire again, my texts beginning with "Tell Jessica this," and "What did she say?" It would have been easier if we just duked it out ourselves over the phone and left out the middle man. Even through text, Jessica maintained her stoic nature and the control. This time, though, I knew she was going back to Florida, so I wanted the control this time. I was at a family dinner at the time, texting underneath the tablecloth at the restaurant. My mom whispered, "Put the phone away!" sharply under her breath. Usually, I had good table manners, but nothing was more important to me than getting in the last word. I never got her phone number, but I didn't want it anymore. The great sunshine state of Florida got in our way, or my way. I don't know why Jessica didn't want to have any contact with me after she moved. Maybe she saw it as an opportunity to rid herself of my emotional eleven-year-old burden.

I was visibly upset after our text-argument ensued. I was even more confused after receiving the texts from Jessica, through

Claire, explaining that Jessica just didn't want to talk to me anymore. The one thing she left out in her message to me was *why* she didn't want to talk to me anymore. On the car ride home from the restaurant, I sat thinking about what I had done to push away my first friend.

So, when middle school started, Jessica wasn't one of the girls that I squeezed on the lunch bench with. She was in Florida, probably wearing shorts year-round and going to Disney World every day, at least that's what I assumed.

Eventually, Claire and I grew apart, too. Although just as emotional as me, she had the same ability to control. Whenever I told her that she made me feel bad, she would do a 180 and turn the whole thing on me, until I was sending a flurry of apologetic texts and she was the one who forgave me. I guess it was a defense mechanism, switching the blame back on the other person when confronted. But eventually it backfired. One time, when we were in the middle of a fight about something I probably did, my family hosted our annual Super Bowl party. I always invited Claire over the past few years. We had a bunch of neighborhood families over, and while the parents watched the game, the kids would hang out in the basement running around and eating my Dad's homemade wings (a recipe from a popular Johnstown joint). Since we were in the middle of a fight, I invited my friend Aliya instead. After the party was the first time Claire had ever apologized to me.

"I'm sorry," she said to me as we walked to the bus that would take us home from school. "I should have apologized earlier."

"Why?" I asked. I was taken aback, I had never heard her say she was sorry to me. I lifted my head a little higher. I had the control now.

"You know—the party. I should've apologized," she said. I knew what she meant. She wished she would have apologized earlier for the sole reason to come to the Super Bowl party and eat my dad's delicious homemade wings.

"Oh," I said. I didn't say it was fine, because I knew she didn't actually feel bad for hurting my feelings. But I kept my head lifted, because I had the leftover homemade wings in my fridge and she would have to wait until next year.

After my friendship with Claire dwindled to only an acknowledgment in the hallway, I was able to focus on my lunch table friends. The ones who gradually came to squeeze on the bench that was meant for three people but stretched to fit four or even five when someone was bumped from another table. It was always a risk to leave your seat in the middle of lunch. Since our school was so large and they shoved 500+ kids in a lunchroom, it took some students half the period just to get their mediocre food.

This was mid-Obama administration, so the healthy lunch campaign was in effect, causing complaints of tasteless food and boring vegetables. Although Michelle Obama probably had good intentions with getting healthier meals in schools, it didn't stop me from getting a cinnamon Pop Tart from the vending machine every day at lunch. I can't think of anything more processed than a Pop Tart—I have no idea what makes up the filling or how they make the icing, but it sure is a great reward for sitting through an hour of Algebra. I would always tell my friends to guard my spot at the lunch table while I go deposit my seventy-five cents in the vending machine. Everything else in the vending machine was fifty cents, only the Pop Tart was worth the extra quarter, but I didn't care. (My mom always told me I had expensive taste.) If I was lucky I would still climb into my seat when I retrieved my treat, but sometimes, someone had shoved themselves on the end of the table, forcing me to squeeze my cheeks onto an even smaller space in between two girls.

I probably learned more about the world at my lunch table than I did in my World Cultures or History class. I swear we had at least one person representing a certain type of religion or race or belief at that lunch table. I had a Pakistani Muslim friend, an Indian Sikh friend, a Korean friend, a Chinese friend, a Taiwanese friend (she was only there for week, but I still count her) an Irish Protestant friend, an atheist friend, a half-Afghani and half-Finnish friend (who would later become by best friend in high school), and a whole slew of white friends with various European backgrounds. At that lunch table was where I also met a Democrat for the first time, at least her family was Democrat. We argued one day about whether Romney or Obama was the better candidate as if we were defending the honor of our family beliefs. We had no idea what we were talking about when it came to politics. (I still don't and don't think anybody does.) Nonetheless, we debated like we were experts until the bell rang. The next day, we were shoulder to shoulder again.

My other friend, Hovni, had hair longer than the whole table combined. She kept it in two braids in elementary school, and then moved it all to one side braid in middle school. As many young girls are, we were always fascinated by her long, thick hair. Hovni was a take-no-crap type of person, and when anyone would ask her a dumb question about her hair, she would shut it down before they could let out a chuckle. Our friend Nicole and I would take her braid and slap each other with it, sometimes even using it to hit Hovni herself. It seems culturally insensitive when looking at it now, but whenever we took her hair as a weapon, she would hit us right back. (Sometimes with her hand, like I said—take-no-crap.) Whenever Nicole and I would visit Hovni's house, we would see her Indian culture past her hair. Although living in America, Hovni still had an undeniable loyalty to her home country. Indian movies were often playing on her living room TV. She would take quick glances while we were eating, saying "This part is so sad!" or talking about how cute a character was.

Nicole, Aliya, another friend of ours, and Hovni were all my main friends in middle school. They also lived close to me, only a neighborhood behind and sometimes they would come to play Mulchman with Claire, Jessica, and me. We would take turns going to each other's houses and meeting at that park that was in between all of us. Nicole was always giggly. She always talked about how she hated her laugh, but it was always the signal that everything was going fine and was the kick starter in all the conversations I remember between the four of us. Aliya, on the other hand, was wonderfully bonkers while we were in middle school. In elementary school, she was painfully quiet, and barely held conversations with me or other people in class, but in middle school her demeanor changed. It was when we all became closer and I think we drew the crazy right out of her. In middle school she was energetic and the cause of many of Nicole's fits of giggles. Sometimes, for reasons I still don't know, she would randomly make a strange, loud sound out of nowhere. She would also steal our iPods when we weren't looking and take hundreds of photos of her making weird faces from odd angles. We would always keep at least some of them for blackmail later. Our philosophy was if you take a photo on my iPod, you give me permission to post it anywhere.

All of us ended up going to different high schools. Nicole went to our zoned high school, Hovni went to a different magnet school than I did, and Aliya went to private school. We don't see each other nearly as much now and we don't meet at the park anymore to play Mulchman. Even though our friendship was like a quilt with mis-matched patterns stitched all over it, we still worked together cohesively. Although our beliefs differed greatly from each other, ironically, they were the only ones I could completely confide in, telling them all that was happening in my seemingly overwhelming life.

I haven't talked to Jessica or Claire in a few years. Sometimes I imagine what it would be like if they'd stuck around. If we'd worked out all the kinks and stayed the close friends we were when we were little. If we did, I may not have been as close with my strange quilt group, or maybe I wouldn't have even sat at that sardine-packed table at lunch. A few years ago, there were many times where I wished I could show Jessica and Claire how much I'd grown and how much they missed out on me as a person. I spent many times thinking that they owed their friendship to me, and that they broke an unspoken promise to stay friends forever like we all saw in TV shows. But nothing is like that, no matter how we want it to be. It just ends up in a big pile of dirty socks.

9. Leaving Rehoboth

Every summer, sometime in the middle of July, my mom, dad, sister, and I would pile groceries and suitcases into our golden Honda minivan until my Dad couldn't look out the back window. We were on our way to Rehoboth Beach, Delaware, where we would meet the rest of our family for a week. My sister, Olivia, and I were bubbling with anticipation on the car ride, excited to see our cousins and dive into the humongous waves of the Atlantic Ocean. I assume my parents were just as ready to get there, just to make our unceasing questions of how close we were to stop. The drive was just over two hours, but every minute felt endless to a child who can't sit still for half a second. However, all my fidgeting would end once I saw the huge white water tower that read "Rehoboth Beach" in blue letters. It was the sign that told me "You're here" and the moment when my parents would flip through MapQuest pages trying to figure out where to go to get to the house we were renting.

"Slow down here, you're going to miss the turn," my mom said, directing my Dad through Rehoboth. My mother, although kind and compassionate, was a grade-A backseat driver.

She could direct a blind man through traffic with the way she talks when my Dad is the one driving. We were coming up on the next stoplight, and my Dad still wasn't in the left lane.

"Craig! You have to turn! Get in the left lane," said my Mom. I can't remember exactly what happened, but I'm sure my Dad sped into the left lane and my Mom yelled a few more times.

"Do you think everyone else is there yet?" I asked, trying to cut the tension. My parents are both quiet and calm people but driving brought out the worst in each of them. As their child, I thought the only thing that could make them stop fighting over driving was to remind them that I, their lovely child, was still in the car.

"I don't know, honey," my mom responded. Olivia was still asleep.

We were always the second family to the house. Once my dad pulled up to the house we were renting, and I yanked my little suitcase out of the pile of stuff in our trunk, my sister and I would sprint to find the best room in the house. When we first started going to the beach, we rented this one house on Maryland Avenue. Being so young, I can only remember certain parts of what the house looked like. There was a blue couch with colorful patterns and flower-like designs all over it. It was so prominent that I could never forget it even if I wanted to. The couch was quite ugly; it looked like someone sewed an off-brand Lilly Pulitzer dress on it and thought it would be perfect for a beach house. The couch was especially good for rainy days, when my cousins and I would squeeze on it watching a movie on a portable

DVD player. It was also a beautiful part of our family photos; when we all stood on the staircase, it sat right below the railing, its bright blue fabric peeking through on the bottom of the frame. It was in the background of another photo, where I stood in my leopard print bathing suit with my Nana's leopard print hat on my head and a wide toothy smile.

I also remember the dumpster that was outside the house and a little way down the sidewalk. It was right before we got onto the boardwalk and on the path we took to get to the beach. The dumpster reeked so bad, that if I even think about it, I can smell the stench. My dad would hoist me up on his shoulders and I would hold my nose as we walked by, hoping to avoid whatever was in that dumpster that made it smell so awful.

Eventually, we all wanted a change in scenery, so the Goodwin family vacation made a move from Rehoboth Beach to the Outer Banks. We could afford a bigger house down there, but it still didn't compare to the crowded beaches of Delaware, so we went back, but to a different house than the one on Maryland Avenue. By this time, my cousins were teenagers, and the eldest was already in college. But that didn't stop us from having our annual "Kids' Night." Every year, all the cousins would go out for Grotto Pizza together, mini golf on the roof, and play games at Funland. Grotto pizza was *the* pizza place at Rehoboth Beach, with one on every block. We would often go as a whole family at least a couple of times. But kids' night was always the highlight since I could be with the older cousins who were so cool to a younger Lauren. Every young child wants to be older than they are at the time, and I was no different. After we were stuffed with pizza and gelato our next stop was Ryan's Mini Golf on the roof, where you could play a whole game of mini golf for only four (now five) dollars. At the very last hole, you would try to hit your ball into a clown's nose. If you were successful, then you won a free game of mini golf. Usually, at least one of us would win—to this day it has never been me—and they would save it a whole year to use on the next trip to Rehoboth.

After we finished our game, the six of us would play the over-priced and rigged games at Funland. It was a mini amusement park on the board walk with typical fair games and rides that never changed. There were rides like the frog-hopper, which was my favorite until I almost got sick while on it, the pirate ship, which I never got on because I was too scared, the haunted house, which I got on even though I was too scared to appease my father. And lastly there was the gravitron, a big UFO looking structure that spun so fast the gravity went all wacky. I still refuse to go on the gravitron ever since I heard a story that someone who went on it got sick, and because of the messed-up gravity, their own vomit smacked them in the face.

My cousins and I would avoid the rides. They were probably dirty with the grimy hand prints of children on vacation and you could never hear the person in the ticket booth anyway, so there was no point. We played the typical fair games; pay two or three bucks and you get to play against other strangers for a prize that probably wasn't worth the money. One year, my sister and the second-eldest cousins Kristen and Kelsey and I got sucked into the wormhole that is the horse race game. At the game, one would roll a ball and try to get it into the farthest hole, similar to skee-ball, this would make your horse travel the most distance. The better you did, the faster your horse went, thus causing you to win the race. The game was a hit among beach goers. We would often stand by a crowd of people waiting to steal a seat in the game. The game was organized so that if you win two small prizes you can trade it in for a medium. Once you get two mediums you can trade in for a large and then an extra-large. The extra-large prize was a jumbo pillow horse. It hung on the wall of the horse race game booth at the very top of the hierarchy of prizes. Most would look at the huge prize and scoff at its uselessness and unattainability. And that's normally what our family would do, but this year, something changed, and we all wanted the coveted stuffed prize, no matter the price.

Every day Kristen, Kelsey, Olivia, and I would walk down the boardwalk, normally around evening time when the game was full, so we'd get the biggest size prize possible. We would play countless horse race games, treating it like a Sunday football game, cheering on whoever was playing at the moment. We celebrated when one of us would win, and then we'd play another one, hoping to win as many times as possible to be able to trade in for the next biggest prize. Eventually, we all had won enough games that all four of us had a large prize. But we continued playing until our seemingly unattainable goal of beating the rigged amusement park game was achieved. After asking for change numerous times, telling our parents to play, and more cheering each other on, we all had the mother of all prizes. I was the last one to attain it. It was on the second to last day of our trip and we took a picture of all of us together holding our crowning achievement. We were proud that we fooled the notorious fair game, but if we counted up all the money we spent on just the horse game that week, it would probably reveal that the game in fact fooled us.

That was one of the last years that the whole family was at Rehoboth Beach. Kristen and Kelsey were at the tail end of high school. So was my other cousin Jonny, and Elizabeth, the oldest, was in college on the way to becoming a teacher. Everyone was growing up and no one really had time to go to the beach with extended family anymore. It was a hard truth for a younger me to face; I didn't understand that people had to grow up. I wanted so desperately to stay in my beachy Neverland and just couldn't grasp what was so hard about leaving home for a week.

I am one of the last of the Goodwin cousins to leave Rehoboth Beach. My sister will follow me in two years. Growing up hit me like a strong wave, sending me tumbling to the shore, with sand in my hair and salt water in my lungs. It shocks my family too. "I can't believe she's already [insert age here]," says a multitude of relatives at family gatherings. It's hard to face the fact that I am in the spot that my cousins once were a few years ago. We talk about it over Thanksgiving and Easter dinners, wondering over how the youngest won't seem so young anymore. All of us cousins gather around a foldable table in my grandmother's dining room, aptly named "the kids' table" even though, technically, my sister Olivia and I are the only kids, and the eldest is even married now. (Her husband joins us at the kids' table too.) We talk about whatever is going on in our lives from sports to new jobs while eating as much ravioli and meatballs as we could muster. Occasionally, we overhear laughter and quiet conversation from the larger "adult" table next to us and eavesdrop to see who the whispers were about. It was a typical family affair, surrounded by way too many meatballs and dinner rolls (which I hoarded), turkey, and vegetables (which I avoided) and plenty of banging on the table laughter.

After the passing of my grandfather, it gradually became harder to gather the family in Johnstown, Pennsylvania, where my Dad and his brothers grew up. We meet at each family's house, taking turns hosting Easter and Thanksgiving and trying to meet for Christmas two months late. With worries about my grandmother being alone three hours away from any family, in the near future, our connection to Johnstown will be lost. And with my grandmother down in Maryland, there would be no point in taking the trek up to Johnstown. Losing Rehoboth beach was hard, but the very house my Dad grew up in? The house that would fill my head with excitement on the long car ride from Baltimore? How could any of us let that piece of our family go? There would no longer be crowding in the living room to watch the Thanksgiving football game or waiting anxiously at the door for my cousins to arrive. We wouldn't wait an hour for those coveted Johnstown wings at the infamous Murphy's, crowded around a table in the corner of the tiny restaurant teeming with people. There wouldn't be any Sunday mornings at St. Benedict's Church, listening to Father Pallis's calming and compassionate voice read us the Gospels.

I've thought about how painful it would be to clean out my grandmother's home completely. We'd have to rid all the walls of her paintings signed "L. Goodwin," written on the corner of each portrait or landscape. We would take all the Crucifixes and religious quotes from the wall. (Which would take hours). The pictures of my dad and his brothers when they were young would come down, packed away in a separate box to send with my grandmother to her new home. I couldn't bear to see the room that I stayed in empty for the last time. The room was the first door to the left when you walked down the hallway that extended from the living room. A small twin bed was pushed up against the wall, with a white metal frame and colorful quilt the colors of Easter—the type of bed you only find in your grandmother's house. That was where I slept. My sister slept on a trundle bed that we would pull out from under the twin bed when we arrived at her house and push back under when we were packing up to leave. Seeing the floor so bare and empty of a mattress with wrinkled sheets was the sign that we were leaving. Without us there, there was no one to sleep there. Anyone can push back the trundle with ease, but thinking about moving the mattress one last time, leaving it like that forever, makes the task seem impossible.

Although I was the last of the family to leave Rehoboth, my grandmother will be the last to leave Johnstown, leaving behind a trail of memories and beginning a new cycle of rotating

Thanksgiving and Easters. Two homes left to someone else, unaware of the three generations that gathered there.

10. Stained Glass Windows

Stained glass windows are my sunsets. The kind you see driving home from your grandmother's house one evening, when you look out the window out of sheer boredom. It is a melting whirlpool of yellows, oranges, and pinks, rising above a highway or residential homes, a sky line or a shopping center. Simply put, it is beautiful, so you take out your phone to snap a photo, but it comes out grainy, muted, and underwhelming, a lame landscape, far from the masterpiece in the sky. Taking a picture can never capture the moment a sun sets. It's like imitating Picasso. You just can't do it. That's what it's like with stained glass windows. They can probably be recreated with hard work. But the feeling you get when the sun hits them just right, that one moment, can't be captured in the lens of a camera.

It is those times I go to Mass on Saturday evenings instead of Sunday mornings, when the days are a little shorter, and the sun seems to descend faster, filtering through the stained-glass windows of St. Joseph Church, casting a warmth over the congregation that I feel the most myself, the fullest. I am never hungry on those Saturday evenings, nor thirsty, nor tired. It is my sunset on a car ride home, when nothing matters except what is before me.

I stand, sit, and kneel, going from reverence to reverence, beneath the beautiful images of our Lord at his most trying and triumphant times; His glory shines through the colored glass, and He stands before me in his true presence at the altar. I am stolen from the Earth and taken to peace. It is love personified in a song, a celebration, and a window. It is the promise that is never broken, from birth to death, from dark to light, from serpent to saint. The stained-glass windows are my looking glass, giving me a glimpse of Heaven, a glimpse of God, of Jesus crowned with thorns, the light shining through His face.

At closing prayer, that line from earth to eternity seems to fade away. I am thrust into a world that no longer feels just right anymore. I walk out of St. Joe's, into the sun that once cradled me through the stained-glass and am forced to see it without a lens of comfort. The sun has set. It is night. I wish to say that leaving Mass is easy and the love felt in the pews carries out over into the real world, but the harsh reality of the secular world enters the mind, wringing dry my sense of hope. How can I be as strong as our Lord in those windows? The sun shines through the stained-glass windows, and casts a warmth over the congregation, but what if I am not there? What if I stay home next week? What if I choose the road most traveled?

Choosing the narrow road to Heaven is easy. At least when you think you know what is going to happen. Choose God, love Him, love everyone, don't sin, get to Heaven. Easy, just like a project; finish and you dust your hands off, admiring the fantastic work you've done on life. This is not the case; when imperfect beings follow a perfect God, the road gets windy and rough. My road to heaven hasn't always been the warm moments at our parish.

Most of my prayer is sloppy. Kind of like handwriting at the end of a long essay, just trying to squeeze those last few words in. Most of the time I pray at my desk, with Scripture, written Catholic prayers, devotionals, or sometimes just talking to God like He's right in front of me. I get distracted a lot, start thinking about what homework I have to do tomorrow, or how I will talk to this person or teacher, or what stupid thing I said during the day. Everything works against me when I pray, even my own brain. I try to corner myself at my brown wooden desk in my room, with only the desk lamp as light. Any other light is too bright, too distracting. I try to focus, squeeze my eyes, and force everything unimportant out of my mind, to leave the most room possible for the most important. But no amount of space in my brain is ever big enough for God, and eventually some thought comes creeping back in, and I am knocked out of that transcendence, just like that closing prayer at Mass.

Everything working against me. Makes sense when talking about distraction in prayer but seems like an exaggeration when talking about life. But living in a world that has forgotten God, the very thing that holds me together, makes it a little harder to live out the faith. I long to be in the confines of those stained-glass windows, with nothing to distract me, no one to tell me what to believe, and no wall between me and my Lord.

I sit at my brown wooden desk at the end of the day, cluttered with papers crumpled and folded, random objects scattered about the surface. I shove them somewhere out of my sight to deal with later and the ten o' clock blues hit me all over again, filling my mind with doubts of what I did or said at that one time or place. God wraps his ever-present arms around me, holding me until I am half-alright. Anyone can tell me that everything is going to be alright, but the only one who really knows with absolute certainty is God. Sometimes, I don't feel God's arms, or I don't even feel like He is there at all. But giving up my control to Him makes handling all of the mess fall from my grasp and into His.

Nothing is my biggest fear. It used to be loneliness, but nothingness tops it by a thousand. Nothing means nobody, but it also means no earth, no smiling, no happiness. No brown wooden desk, no mother to tell you how proud she is of you. No pencils, no pancakes, no puppies. No aunts, uncles, or sisters. Or cousins on Thanksgiving. No sunsets. No stained glass. No God.

The universe came out of nothing. That's how everything began. There was nothing, then there was something. A potter takes a slab of clay, and puts in on the potter's wheel, molding it and shaping it with delicate fingers until there is something. I like to think that's how God made me, taking a misshapen chunk of clay, and molding it into what He wants me to be. A mole on her left cheek, no taller than 5'3, same face as her mom, really soft on the inside, and the same on the outside.

On the bus ride to school, I try to take out my rosary. It

sits at the bottom of the smallest pocket on my backpack. I stuff my hand in, and grab the shiny wooden beads, pulling it out between tangled headphones and hair ties. The rosary makes it halfway out before someone walks by, their head scouring the seats for an open spot to sit. They point to the empty space next to me, asking if they can sit. I nod, move my things, and stuff myself into the corner, putting my rosary back into the tangles of my backpack pocket. I have ten fingers, the same number of beads on the rosary. I count the Hail Mary's on my fingers, making the sign of the cross really tiny with my index finger on my stomach. We pass by St. Joe's on the way to school. I make the sign of the cross again, trying to touch my forehead this time to make it a little more real. I go back to counting the Hail Mary's on my fingers, not my rosary beads, reflecting on the mysteries of Christ. Whenever I remember to pray it, it is usually on a Tuesday or Friday, the days to pray the sorrowful mysteries. I pray them, never taking out my beads.

I'm back at my wooden desk. I didn't finish that rosary. I only said one decade and I got really distracted so I took out my headphones and listened to music the rest of the way. "At least I got a decade in, that's better than nothing," I say to myself. "I'll do better tomorrow," I say to myself again, God too. I ask Him to help me. To make everyone walk past me on the bus so I can sit alone. So I can use the actual rosary instead of my fingers. Maybe using the necklace will make me focus more on the prayer and less on the brake lights reflecting in the window. Or on my homework that's due tomorrow, or on the kid sitting next to me and what he's listening to on his headphones. Maybe I should leave my headphones home. They usually distract me too. But then I can't listen to music on the way home. I'll just bring them, then I can listen to the Foo Fighters during lunch. Or that new album, by that one guy who was on the Voice. I wonder if I can buy lunch tomorrow. I'm tired of eating sandwiches every single day. I have English before lunch so I can't do my homework then. Crap, I have to read three chapters before next class. What else do I have to do? Read chapters, do math problems, write that thing for lit, science paper, third draft of article, redo the quiz before Thursday, so much to do before Thursday; God help me pray the rosary tomorrow.

Confession is from 3:00 to 4:00 on Saturdays in the church. I get off work at 2:00, then I eat, maybe take a ten-minute nap, then I'm back in the car, driving to St. Joe's once more. Only a few cars sit in the parking lot. The car with the Perry Hall Music sign on the side sits in the first spot as always, never moving. I get out of the car and walk across the parking lot, opening the brown wooden door to the entrance. The pews are empty, but to my right a line of people wait silently. I dip my hand in the holy water; sometimes I forget since there is no Mass to attend today. I stand at the end of the line and pull the tiny prayer book out of my purse, a wrinkly yellow post it note marking the Act of Contrition, a prayer I still can't recite from memory, or won't, for fear that I'll mess it up and the priest will make me say my sins all over again. The church is cold. They always keep the air conditioning on high. I don't know why.

Every five or so minutes someone walks out of the confessional, and we all move up. The praise and worship band practices for the evening Mass, playing hymns and songs of worship to an empty church. I focus on the stained-glass windows waiting to see if the light will hit them just right, but it's too early. The church feels quiet even when the band is playing. It is a good kind of quiet; not the absence of sound but the presence of peace. Someone walks out. Five minutes closer to confession. Sometimes this is the only quiet I get. At school or at home there may be silence, but never quiet. There is always something going on, something to do or say, someone to break the silence. But here, everything is quiet, even my mind. I'm next. I look over the Act of Contrition once more, pray to God that he helps me remember everything I did wrong over the past month. The worst feeling is when you leave and forgot to confess something; it's still forgiven, but it doesn't feel the same. It shouldn't be long now until I tell the holiest person I know all the terrible things that I've done. Sometimes I wonder why God needs us to tell others our sins to be forgiven. Why couldn't I just tell God directly and skip the middle man? That's not how it works, most people tell me. I get it. God is everywhere, and he already knows what I've done wrong, but if I have to tell a priest my sins to be forgiven then there is a high chance that I probably won't do them again to save me the embarrassment. Eventually, the embarrassment part fades some, and you start worrying more about God in the room rather than the priest in the room. It's really smart the way He set things up. The door clicks open, a smile from the confessor, the smile of a clean soul. I walk in, my thumb in my little prayer book on the Act of Contrition page, and purse held against my waist. I sit in the chair in front of the priest.

I begin. My nerves aren't prominent whenever I walk in, but something always causes both my leg and my voice to shake. It's that last minute hesitation, self-doubt. *Could God really forgive me?* I turn my face down, focusing on the carpet in the small room, and fidget with my book, not making eye contact, like a child apologizing to a parent for misbehaving. I let my eyes wander, trying to focus on anything but the robed man in front of me. The room is dim, lit by a ceiling light and a small lamp beside my chair. No light flows in through the door; the main church lights haven't been turned on yet. I continue to confess. Father has his eyes closed, but I know he is listening. He nods his head, his hands folded. He looks to be in deep thought, like he's praying. Maybe he's praying for me. I hope so; I need it. Long pauses fill the space between my sins. The things I've done or failed to do are fleeting; they run away from my mind, somewhere deep within my conscience, not wanting to come to the surface, to let the air hit them. I say what is there, hoping God will know the rest—His memory is better than mine. "I think that's it." is always my line to let the priest know when I am done. There is nothing left for me to say, and it's his turn—and then God's turn—to talk.

Father breathes deeply. He always does this, but I always think he sighs because he is overloaded with all the terrible things that I've done and doesn't know what to do with me. Then, he begins to speak.

95

"Well, let's thank God for a good and humble confession." He always says this too, and my mind calms down again. My shoulders un-shrug themselves, letting go of the stress that I took in with me to the confessional. I breathe deeply now, as if to expel all the sins I just put in the air, to blow them out of the door and all the way outside, into the cemetery, where they decompose and disintegrate back into the soil, never to be heard again. Father still has his eyes closed as he gives me his penance. Even though he's talking, he still seems to be praying.

"Now, go ahead and make your Act of Contrition," says Father, another thing he always says. I open my book, my thumb already on the page with the wrinkled post it note and recite the prayer. My words fill with anticipation. I'm this close to forgiveness, and God is in front of me, waiting. Father finally extends his hand over me to absolve my sins. I lean forward a little, trying to catch as much blessing as I can. I make the sign of the cross, this time big and bold, across my chest and way up to my forehead.

"Go in peace," Father says to me. "Pray for me," he adds as I get up and walk towards the door.

"Of course," I say and open the door, leaving the door half-open behind me for the next person. I smile, that smile of a clean soul, and sit in an empty pew to say my penance. God is still in front of me, but He needs not to wait. He sits next to me and beside me in the pew, stands tall in the tabernacle, and holds onto my heart, never letting go.

It is evening. I am in the back seat on the driver's side,

on the way home from my grandparent's house. The sun is setting, and I am reading. I look up every few minutes, to give my eyes a rest and to prevent from getting a headache. My sister is beside me, my mom in front of her, my dad driving, and the sun setting. Mom points out the sunset, the pinks and oranges fading together in between the fast-moving trees of rural Maryland. I take a break and look; it's beautiful. God is in that sunset, too.

11. High Heels

I bought my first pair of heels in Johnstown, Pennsylvania. I was probably around six or seven years old and I thought heels were only meant for women and I was still just a girl. I was in some big department store with my grandparents. It was either a Ross, Boscov's, or a JCPenney. I can't remember which. We were in the shoe section with tall racks towering over me, each aisle representing a different size shoe. We were walking through with a purpose, of which I can't remember, probably to find some nice church shoes or something to wear while we were visiting. If my mom didn't go shopping with us she would always give us an objective, so we wouldn't pick up everything and throw it in the cart. By that time, my sister and I figured out that anyone who wasn't our parent would buy us anything we wanted as long as it wasn't outrageously expensive, and we gave them a big smile.

Such was the case for my grandparents. We were also the youngest of their six grandchildren, easily making us the most spoiled in our family. I can't remember what my parents were doing that day that caused our grandparents to take us shopping to keep us occupied. I had a very short attention span as a child (I still do) and I wouldn't pay attention to anything that wouldn't excite me. That day the only thing I could focus on were the beautiful pair of white lace wedges that were sitting at the very top of the shoe rack in the department store. Everything else faded into the background like it does when a man sees a beautiful woman in the movies.

I never had a pair of heels before; I only wore sweaty pairs of flats with bright white tights when I had to dress nice. Sometimes I would go into my mom's long closet and try on her heels, walking around like I was a movie star on the red carpet. Her closet was like a long hallway, perfect for strutting. Clothes lined the side of the walls and wrapped around the back of it. If we were getting ready to go somewhere I would sneak into her closet after I was done (my getting ready consisted of brushing my hair twice on each side and half-putting my clothes on) and pull out all of her high heels while I was waiting for her. They were on these tiny slanted racks lining the wall on the floor. I would pull them off and place them on my feet; the big gap between the heel of my foot and the heel of my mom's shoe was quite comical, but it didn't stop me from feeling like a million bucks. I had always been the shortest girl in my grade and even though the heels were about four inches tops, I felt like I could tower over all the girls blessed with the tall gene.

Eventually, after I had made a mess of her closet, I would strut out to show Mom how grown up I was. She would look at me and smile, saying I looked beautiful, and then she would see the mess I made of her closet. I had a real bad habit as a kid of taking everything out of its spot and then never putting it back and it drove my mother crazy. (It still does, I'm sorry Mom.)

Wearing my mom's heels made me feel important. To me, Mom was the prettiest woman I knew. I wanted to be like her in every way—wear her shoes, curl my hair, and put on lipstick. Growing up, my mom was (and still is) the woman I look up to the most. She was feminine and beautiful; stern, yet motherly. Putting on her shoes made me feel more like her, which subsequently made me feel more like a woman.

Despite my growing affection for the high-fashion shoe, I still never had a pair of my own. The moment I saw those white wedges I knew I wanted them more than anything that I had desired before. I looked up at the very top rack, my little eyes wide. The top of the rack was like the top of a mountain, its peak my prize. I pointed to the top rack asking my grandfather to take them down, so I could try them on. I was afraid that they would say no outright since they were heels and I was too young to wear them. Nevertheless, he got them and placed them in my hand.

"Can I try them on?" I asked my grandparents with the widest smile possible.

"Yeah, go ahead," one of them said. I can't remember who since I was too focused on the shoes.

I plopped down right there in the middle of the aisle and started taking off my shoes. I slid the shoe on my foot as elegantly as I could. I spent a minute or two trying to figure out how to tighten them, my nubby fingers not being able to adjust the strap. The shoes fit perfectly. My biggest worry was seeing these shoes and having them not fit me at all; I had terribly tiny feet and not a lot of shoes could fit me.

I sat on the floor lifting my foot up and turning it side to side to let my sister and grandparents see how good it looked. I looked up at them with pleading eyes, asking them if I could get them.

"I don't know if your mother will like you wearing heels," my grandmother said.

"We can always return them!" I said. I was quick to respond. I had any excuse to get those shoes into my grasp even if it meant turning them over later. I flashed them my best smile— it didn't take much to convince them to buy it for me. I remember standing in line watching my first pair of high heels being checked out, the cashier not knowing the milestone she was helping take part in. There was still a small fear in the back of my mind that my mom would make me return them, but the excitement of the moment was enough to override any fear of what could happen when we got back to my grandparent's house.

My first pair of heels was the beginning of my passage into womanhood. It seems dramatic that a pair of shoes would mark my entering into a new type of maturity, but that's exactly what it was. Going to high school or opening my first checking account or even getting my license never gave me that sense of "grownup-ness" that I felt when I slid my foot into a pair of heels. I had closed the gap between the heel of my foot and the heel of my shoe and with that I no longer had to dress up in my mother's fancy heels.

When we got home, I showed my mother my new pair

of heels. I even tried them on for her, so she could see how great they looked. To my surprise at the time, she let me keep them without me having to do any major convincing. All it took was one smile and she said yes. Looking back, I know that there was no reason for her to take those shoes back, and it was just the paranoia in my kid brain.

My spike in maturity that day is one of the major milestones that marks my beginning in embracing all things feminine. In the moment I put on the white wedges, my womanhood started piecing itself together like a puzzle. I can't remember where I wore those heels for the first time, but I know I felt like a true woman, Not a girl, but a woman.

Growing up we all go through phases and almost all of mine were feminine. In middle school, I convinced myself that I was going to get my cosmetologist license and open a salon when I got out of school. I had watched countless tutorials on intricate braids and nail art to practice. Each morning before I went to school, I would stand in my bathroom mirror, the sink cluttered with hair ties and bobby pins, trying to recreate some hairstyle. Ultimately, I would fail and throw my hair up in a ponytail. My mom would always tell me to keep my hair down since it seemed like almost every day I wore it up in a ponytail. It was only because after messing with it so much, my hair looked like some wild animal had slept in it and the only way to make it look decent was to put it in a ponytail and loop it around once, making it look like a saggy bun on the top of my head.

For Christmas one year my mom had bought me some

tools for nail art. I spent the whole break from school doing my nails every day, sometimes even twice a day. I would get bored of a design so quickly or get bothered by how one nail turned out bad before I had to take it off. I was the type of person where if there was one chip on one nail, I had to redo the whole thing.

After my stint with being a hair stylist and nail artist, I moved onto makeup. I was never allowed to wear makeup until high school, so I thrived off of my yearly dance recitals; the only time where I could wear a full face of makeup. My mom would do it for me. It was the only time when I wore lipstick. It was bright red, and I asked my mom to reapply it every ten minutes because "I couldn't feel it on my lips anymore." I was afraid if my lipstick had worn off for even a moment that someone might miss out on how beautiful I looked. Dance recitals were the ultimate example of femininity. We all wore brightly colored costumes and crowded into classrooms of the local high school where the recital was held. (We called them dressing rooms.) Our clothes and bags with hangers were all over the place. There was always a "room mom" that would help all the girls get dressed and do their makeup for the show. My mom only did it once and I understand why—we were all loud and energetic from the excitement of the show, and she was the one who had to keep us all in check. The days of the dress rehearsal and the dance recital were days that I looked forward to all year. I remember getting up and putting the costume on for my first dance, having my mom do my makeup and running to the front door to wait impatiently for everyone to be ready to leave. (I was always quick to get ready if where we were going was somewhere I wanted to go.)

When we arrived at the high school and finally got into the room where my class was staying, I would run around trying to find my friends. We would sit in the room eating snacks and watching movies until it was our time to go on stage. The classroom smelled overwhelmingly like hair spray. I never understood why people didn't like the smell. It was the smell of excitement. Hair spray meant it was time for me to showcase all the hard work that I put into this dance all year. Even now when I smell it, I am brought back the high school classroom, my hair stuck with over twenty bobby pins, running around with my fellow dancers trying to get our jitters out.

It wasn't until fifth grade that I started wearing makeup outside of the annual dance show. I had acquired a tube of Skittles-flavored lip gloss somehow and had put it on before school in the morning without telling my mom. She must have known since the shade of the lip gloss was a bright watermelon pink and I really slathered it on until there was a complete layer of goop covering my lips. I wore it because there was a cute boy in my class who (according to another classmate) liked me. She told me one day that he *liked me liked me*. Saying like twice was always suggestive of the "I like you more than a friend" type of like. I wore it pretty much every day that year. It became a sort of superstition to me. I had convinced myself that if I stopped wearing the lip gloss, he wouldn't like me anymore. That was the first time I put pressure on myself to be beautiful. Eventually, I found out that he didn't like me anymore (not in the like like way at least) and I stopped wearing the Skittles-flavored lip gloss.

As I grew older my mom slowly started letting me wear more makeup. I started wearing mascara sometime in seventh grade, brown pencil eyeliner in eighth grade (only brown—black was too bold) and then in high school I entered full force into the realm of makeup. I had long lost the dream of being a hair, nail, and makeup artist, but that didn't stop me from buying every form of makeup I could find.

I bought my first eyeshadow palette with an Amazon gift card on the internet. It was from the brand Lorac Pro, and it was expensive. I had never owned high-end makeup before, but it was what everybody used in the videos, so I thought it was the only way to get better. I tracked the package on my phone the whole week, watching where it was at every moment of the day. I got the notification that it was delivered when I was on the bus on my way home from school one day. I felt a surge of the same feeling that I got when I got my first pair of heels. It wasn't the same; I wasn't becoming like anyone I knew personally. When I got my first pair of heels, I was stepping into the shoes of my mother. I felt like I was becoming a woman like my mother—loving, strong, and beautiful. Buying my first item of expensive makeup wasn't like that. I was just becoming older.

Nevertheless, I got off the bus that day, hopped into my mom's car and rode all the way home jabbering about how my makeup palette arrived. I got out of the car and rushed up to the front door to pick up the cardboard box that held my coveted purchase.

That was the start to a long road of more makeup buying and wearing until my pockets were empty of cash and my face caked with foundation. I wore makeup any chance that I got. I wore a full face of foundation, eyeliner, eyeshadow, mascara, blush, contour, and more to school for no reason other than just because. For a long time, I did it because it was fun. It was my art form. I was absolutely terrible at drawing or painting, so painting my face was my way of creating artwork. That eventually changed, and what was a way to express myself soon became a constraint. After a while I became too attached to makeup. It was my validation, and sometimes still is. There were days when I would do my makeup just so I could hear the compliments from my friends. I couldn't go on a trip without packing enough makeup to do my whole face. Even on church retreats I couldn't go out without a little mascara to look a little more like "myself."

The makeup phase finally ended like all the other ones. I still wear it sometimes, but it doesn't bring me the same excitement as it once did when I first wore it at the dance recitals. What was absent from dance recital makeup was the pressure. I was still a little girl, and nobody cared if my red lipstick was a little lopsided on my mouth or if I put a little too much blush on my cheeks. More importantly, I didn't care.

After I started wearing makeup regularly the excitement behind putting it on faded into the clumps of mascara I kept laying on my eyelashes. The need to put it on overpowered the femininity that it gave me. After about a year and a half of trying so hard to make everyone believe I was the perfect woman, I just got lazy. I was tired of waking up early to put on makeup for no other reason that gaining validation from people that may not even care about me.

I don't have my first pair of heels anymore. I didn't keep them in my closet to show my friends or future children. I probably only wore the actual shoe five or six times. I'm sure my mom went through the closets, cleaning out old clothes we didn't wear and saw the shoes. She took them out and held them up to me "Are you going to wear these anymore?" she asked me. I shook my head and watched her dump them in the donate pile. That would be the last I saw of them. The entrance to my femininity was hidden in a pile of Goodwill donations for someone else to buy, maybe for their first pair of heels too. I miss those pair of heels. I've bought a few more pairs since to wear to school dances and parties. Nothing was ever like that first pair of heels, when I stepped into the shoes of many women before me.

12. Camping Memoir #3

After the beloved trailer could no longer host our camp weekends, we had to find a new home for our annual trip. The year after, we decided to try out an actual campground in Frederick, Maryland, but that didn't work out; we were a little too rowdy to share property with other people looking for a peaceful weekend in nature. Not to mention the state park was not beer-friendly, which did not sit well with the dads. (They sneaked some in anyway.) The next year we found out one of the dads had a friend who owned a cabin somewhere in West Virginia and decided to try the place out for a change. We stayed there for camp many years, treating it as our own.

The cabin in West Virginia was off the beaten track quite a bit. Even the town we drove through to get there was bleak; only a Walmart and a few gas stations sat on the desolate road. After driving on windy paths through the woods, past other cabins and sheds, some of which looked trashed and broken beyond fixing, we arrived at the property. There was a small cabin in the center, with a camper parked to the left side of it. To the right was a fire pit and a table, where we would set out all our food for cooking.

We quickly figured out a system as to where everyone

slept; all the girls in the camper and all the dads in the cabin. With the exception of a few girls who slept in a room in the cabin, this was how it always was. The camper quickly became the hub where all the daughters met to play games and just talk about anything. The older girls often played music from a speaker. They played a lot of rap music that, if my mom heard it, she would yell at us to turn it off. After one weekend, I remembered a lot of the artists and songs we listened to—Drake, Lil Wayne, Kanye West, Wiz Khalifa, and more—and my sister and I downloaded them onto my iPod to listen to at home. Of course, my whole family had a shared iTunes account, so when of the rappers was yelling profanities in my dad's ear during a run, he came in and asked who downloaded all the inappropriate music. (My sister told him it was me; I told him it was her.)

Another appealing aspect of the cabin in West Virginia was the dirt hill down the road. On the side of the road was a large hill empty of vegetation except a few weeds and was only covered in dirt and would turn into mud if it rained. One year after a downpour, all of the girls had the great idea of going down to the dirt hill, now the mud hill, and sliding down it. Almost all the girls went. I stayed at the cabin since being covered in mud didn't appeal to me and I wasn't as adventurous as some of the girls. When they came back from the hill, they were covered from head to toe in mud and dirt. Some even had it in their hair. It would be easy to just take off the clothes and hop in the shower, but one of the few rules at camp was no showers, so instead of taking turns hopping in a shower to clean off all the gunk, the girls stood outside while one of the dads hosed them down with water. (I'm sure some of the girls broke the rule and hopped in the shower later to get any lingering mud.)

Although the rain brought mudslides, it also put a damper on some of the plans we had set out to do during the weekend. One year, when rain confined us to the cabin and camper for the first half of the day, all the daughters sat on the porch waiting for it to pass. We thought it would be a great idea to tell scary stories to make the time go faster. I was very easily scared and a worrywart, so anything scary was bound to leave a lasting impact, but I was a sucker for a good story, so I stayed and listened, even though I knew it would cause me nightmares. We told many stories that day, most of which I can't remember. The older girls looked some up on their phones with the little service they had in the middle of nowhere.

One of the stories was about a young girl who was babysitting for a couple, when she saw a clown statue in the room where she was watching the kids. The clown statue was creeping her out, so she called the couple to ask if she could cover it up. When the couple answered, they told her they didn't own a clown statue, and that was where the story ended. After the abundance of horror stories that day I was thoroughly scared out of my socks, even though it was daylight. It didn't help that the owner of the cabin swore up and down that there was a witch haunting the cabin who took the form of a rabbit. He claims it's true, since he tried shooting this same rabbit multiple times, and each time it went away unscathed. Later at night, in the camper, I lay with my eyes wide open, staring out the window, hoping a crazy serial killer wouldn't come in and kill us all. It was an irrational fear, but these stories had to come from somewhere, right? For almost a whole year after hearing the scary stories at camp I had nightmares and constantly worried about experiencing one of the insane situations in real life. To this day, I have yet to watch a horror movie.

Not only was there an alleged witch lurking around the cabin, but a small cemetery atop a hill behind the cabin. We had to walk through tons of tall grass and other vegetation to get there. It was a family cemetery with a black fence around it, protecting any animals from getting in. The gravestones were very old, some of the lettering faded so much we couldn't even read what was written. It was interesting to see the cemetery during the day—it was like a piece of history, some of the stones dating back to the late 1800s. This wasn't enough for most of the daughters, though. They decided it would be fun to go visit the cemetery again at midnight. Again, I stayed back at the cabin, too afraid to go when it was pitch black and risk one of those scary stories coming true. So, when the girls embarked on their journey, I stayed seated around the fire. The dads stayed too and came up with a plan to scare the girls when they were walking back from the cemetery. One of the dads had a chainsaw he used to chop wood and a bright orange vest that made him look real creepy. He and one of the other dads went up to the base of the hill and hid, waiting for the girls to come down from the cemetery. Soon enough, I heard the revving of the chainsaw, followed by the screams of the girls then the laughter from the dads. Turns out, my sister and my cousin dove into a nearby bush out of fear and scratched their legs up in the process. It's safe to say I was comfortable sitting by the light of the fire, safe from any chainsaw wielding dads.

After a few years at the West Virginia cabin, another long-time friend of the dads joined. His son, Bryce, around five years old, was now deemed old enough to go. Bryce was another source of entertainment at camp that year. He told these wild stories about his friends' houses catching on fire. We knew they weren't true since his dad never knew a thing about it, but the kid told them as if it happened a week ago. Bryce also loved to make "breakfast sandwiches" every morning instead of eating the food we brought. These "breakfast sandwiches" were just two un-toasted pieces of bread put together with nothing between them.

One morning, while some of us early-risers were sitting by the fire, Bryce walked up from his tent, looking groggy and tired. Someone, I can't remember who, yelled to him, "Hey! What's up Bryce?" Bryce didn't show any enthusiasm, obviously still waking up, and muttered something, which to us, sounded like "soggy fish in my mouth." We didn't understand what he meant, and I don't think he did either. When he plopped himself down by the fire, we asked him why he said that. He shrugged his shoulders and proceeded to make his breakfast sandwich.

Towards the evening, when it was time to eat dinner, all the dads and daughters would gather around the campfire to cook mountain pies (a type of pizza sandwich), hot dogs, hamburgers, and bratwursts. It was usually almost dark by the time we were all by the fire, the sun just descending behind the trees surrounding the cabin. On the cabin porch was a large speaker one of the dads always brought where we blasted music all evening. This was almost always the music taste of the dads, since most of the songs were from before 1990, but daughters liked it too, since we grew up listening to our dads sing them when they came on the radio. Music was always an integral part of camp since it was always playing, and a topic of discussion among all of us. One year, two of the dads had a battle to see who was the best DJ. One of them even went as far to create a DJ name for himself—DJ Vulcan Dragon. I still don't understand what the name meant or why he chose it, but no one questioned it.

One of our favorite songs to listen to at camp was *Take Me Home, Country Roads* by John Denver. When the twangy tune came on everyone who was around would belt out the lyrics, singing our ode to West Virginia. If I ever hear the song outside of camp, I can't stop myself from singing it out loud for everyone else to hear. Many other bands and artists populated the weekend play list—Guns n' Roses, Queen, Counting Crows, Blue Oyster Cult, Van Halen, and any other band that existed in the 80's or earlier.

After it was well into night, all the daughters moved to the camper, and the dads moved to the cabin to play poker. The camper was situated outside the bathroom window, so we heard the shouts of joy and frustration from the game. Sometimes the older daughters would play with the dads, but I never did, even though I was pretty confident in my Texas Hold 'em skills. They played with real money, something I had never done before—

poker chips were all but plastic to me. My dad never won the poker games and was lucky if he broke even, but I knew he never cared.

The daughters would spend our time playing different types of games well into the night. We played card games in the camper until we got bored and played games outside until we were too tired. In the pitch-black night, we would play sardines (a backwards version of hide-and-seek, where when you find someone you hide with them; last person left seeking loses). I remember searching the campground to find someone with my flashlight, hoping I wasn't the last one, the loud music from the speakers still blaring in the background.

Eventually, we moved from the West Virginia cabin, just like we had to move from the trailer. The cabin wasn't torn down or sold. We needed a change in scenery. A few years ago, one of the dads passed away in a tragic accident, something we found out only a few weeks before camp that year. I only saw him once a year, but I knew how much he meant to his daughters and friends. His presence was vibrant and crucial to everything camp was. His vivacity created many memories and stories for all of us. After his passing we moved from West Virginia to a different cabin we rented in Pennsylvania. We continue to go to camp, and remember how lucky we were to have him at camp with us.

We weren't sure where we were going to go the next year, but I don't remember worrying about it. As long as we had a fire pit and some music, camp could be anywhere.

13. Hesitation

I'm sure hesitation is the cause of many great travesties in the modern world. There was probably a great American president who never ran in the election because hesitation was nagging him or her to play it safe. Hesitation always errs on the side of caution. Granted, sometimes hesitation might save a person from doing something stupid, but I'm talking about the voice that says "maybe" while making a decision that is undoubtedly beneficial. Like getting out of bed in the morning (The bed is just too comfortable; five more minutes won't hurt a thing.) Or finishing an assignment. (I have 15 minutes tomorrow morning, that's plenty of time.) Or maybe taking that leap of faith, right into God's arms. (I'm not good enough; He won't want me.)

That little hole of hesitation in my brain is the biggest wall dividing me and the Lord. Hesitation is all my doubts and insecurities jumbled into one large tumbleweed rolling across my consciousness. Sometimes I sit down for prayer and just put my head on my wooden desk, pondering the vastness that is God and the littleness that is me, and how I could possibly fit in His plan for what the world is. Hesitation comes to the forefront of my mind. How could an awesome and all-powerful God love someone as sinful as me? Should I even try anymore?

Hesitation, for me, are those "What's the point?" moments. Why even follow God if I know I am going to screw up anyway? There have been many times I've been reluctant to pray at all, wanting to sort out my mess before I bring it to God.

All my doubt and insecurity built up at one particular Mass. I was at a conference in Indianapolis, aptly named the National Catholic Youth Conference. There were 25,000 other Catholic teenagers who were in attendance, 150 people from the Archdiocese of Baltimore, and only 4 people from my home parish of St. Joseph. (Two of whom were adults.) The whole thing was a little overwhelming, but also a paradise for a young Catholic girl who attended public school. Never in my life was I able to relate to so many people at once.

Before the conference, my prayer life had taken a sharp turn downward. I couldn't stay focused on a prayer for more than thirty seconds and going to Mass, usually the event that I would look forward to all week, became a dreaded affair. Unworthiness constantly clouded my thoughts during the Liturgy, derailing my thoughts and thus making me feel more guilty for not focusing on God. I was determined to get into the right mindset before the conference. To be as holy as I was before so I would really experience God and His love for me.

As expected, I couldn't sort out all the stuff that was going on inside my brain and my heart before the conference. I couldn't force my timing on something that was essentially out of my control. I wanted so desperately to grab a hold of my life in time for the conference, so I could enjoy all the graces that would pour out upon me. I came to the conference with that big tumbleweed of doubt and hesitation still rolling around in my brain collecting dust and dirt as it went.

It was on Friday, the day after we arrived, that we attended daily Mass at the church across the street from the conference center. Before the Mass started, we made our way to the hall where they held confessions. My favorite time to go to confession was at a youth conference or retreat like this one. Confession can be intimidating, but it is a whole lot easier when you're almost 600 miles away from home and know that you're never going to see the priest again. After confession, the first breath I take usually is the sigh of relief, the release of dead and cumbersome weight that I've been carrying over the last month. When I exit the hall where they held confessions, two men greeted me, handing me a sticker with "I'M FORGIVEN" written in big letters on an orange background. I wait outside for my friend and stick the reward on my backpack. I sit in my squeaky-clean state, swimming in the lovely air of forgiveness, knowing that all the dust and dirt that I held for so long was no longer holding me captive.

I wished I had held on to the feeling, that I didn't hesitate to believe God actually forgave me. But after I said my penance, walking down the hall crowded with teens from all over the country, my brain singled in on that one seed of doubt, expanding it to infect every conscious and subconscious part of my brain with hesitation. I was hesitant to trust in God's great gift of mercy.

I was hesitant to open the door God had put right in front of me, and although I was walking to Mass, I wasn't going anywhere.

We made our way out of the conference center, maneuvering our way through the crowds of people exiting and entering, and into the rainy streets of Indianapolis. St. John's was across the street and held five Masses a day to accommodate the influx of teens visiting that weekend. It was drizzling outside, the gray cast of a gloomy day hung over the city. The street that led up to the front of the conference center was littered with food trucks, mostly selling pizza and "world famous" barbecue.

When we opened the tall, ornate doors to the church, it was packed from back to front. Adoration was just closing, and we walked right up to the front of the church to see the Blessed Sacrament leave the altar. We sat down in a short pew on the right side of the church, behind the piano player. My arms were full of random bags and trinkets from booths handing out free items. Quickly, I organized my items, stuffing the random gifts into a bag as quietly as possible before the Mass started. After a minute of shuffling my things in between pockets and shoving things in bags to sort out later, I finally sat down for good, and breathed for the first time since I came out of confession. The church was beautiful. The altar stood elevated, the wall forming a semi-circle surrounding it. Right above it was a miniature dome displaying some holy moment I can't remember; my eyes were flitting around the room too fast. There was a statue of St. Joseph where the singer sat. His normal fatherly pose was a reminder of home.

Seminarians already dressed set up a bunch of folding

chairs surrounding the tabernacle. At least fifteen in total. One stepped down from where the altar stood whispering, to the nearest people in the front pews, "Do you guys want to take up the gifts?" He was met with silence, and stood there for a few seconds, before saying, "Anybody can do it." Finally, a group of people agreed, and he left.

I tried to calm my mind, to get it to stop speeding like a train down a track of thoughts and worries and insecurities. I wanted focus just for a little bit before the Mass started. I was afraid to focus on God, though, because if I focused on God, I focused on everything that was wrong with me. When I was in a state of prayer, all I felt was guilt and when I wasn't in prayer, my mind would go so fast that I couldn't feel it.

Mass began. It was a daily Mass, usually short and concise, but the procession was long since there were multiple priests and bishops who traveled there. Everything in the church that day made me feel little. The grand statue of St. Joseph, the priests stationed to the right of the tabernacle clothed in white vestments, their hands together in what seemed like a perfect prayer. The celebrant of the Mass, the bishop of Lafayette, a neighboring archdiocese of Indianapolis—it isn't often that a bishop celebrates Mass at a local parish. The light that shined through the windows even on the dreary November day. The piano in front of us. The people filling in each pew. It was the feast day of St. Elizabeth of Hungary and although I can't remember much about her, I do know she made me feel little too.

As the Mass progressed, that itching feeling of

unworthiness grew so large it encompassed my whole entire being. My mind was so consumed by my own hurt, that nothing, not even the Eucharist, the source and summit of my faith, could penetrate it. At least, that was my thought at the time. Never had I been so close to completely giving up on prayer. My confession earlier didn't even matter to me; I was still the worst sinner God had ever seen and hesitation won me over. I hesitated to forgive myself, to let the hurt and brokenness go once and for all. I was so overtaken by shame that I felt sick, my body spitting every ounce of insecurity in physical form. I sat down after Communion, closing my eyes in prayer, clenching my hands together as if to force all those terrible thoughts that seeped into even the smallest crevices of my brain. After the bishop closed in prayer we filed out of the church and into the cold and rainy weather once again. I slowly got a grip, but it didn't stop me cursing myself for wasting another Mass.

We went to the crowded food trucks and hopped into the shortest line, waiting in the Indiana dampness for some fish and chips. I pushed that Mass out of my mind—I was good at doing that; ignoring any feeling until it became too great to ignore anymore. We sat, all four of us, on the floor in the hall of the conference center eating our seafood from take-out boxes. I charged my semi-broken phone in the little portable charger I brought, and I ate, talking with my group members, hoping that the next time I talked to God I could fix myself.

The other teenager that went to the conference, AJ, and I made our way to one of the sessions where they give talks about faith. The one we really wanted to go to was already full by the time we got there, so we settled on going to one of the larger sessions with a speaker I already saw at a conference a few years ago. My face fell. I was hoping I could get some new insight that could help me pick up the mess in my brain.

The only thing that was the same as the last time I saw this speaker were the jokes he told (still funny by the way); everything else was new. At the end of his talk, he wanted us to close our eyes and connect with God through our imagination. Fear crept up from behind my back. I have a great imagination but when I am forced to just sit and think my mind wanders, just like in that Mass, and then I can never find my way back. Every time I am forced to sit in a pool of my own thoughts, my mind immediately goes to the negative, telling me that I am not good enough to even talk to God in prayer, and that if I do want to talk to God I need to fix everything wrong with me beforehand. Nevertheless, I was tired of feeling crappy, so I closed my eyes and let the words of the speaker guide me through my imagination.

I am on a mountain and I'm comfortable, but miles away, on top of another mountain, stood Jesus, beckoning me to come over to him. The only problem is that to get there I have to travel through miles of desert and then climb to the peak. The trek down is difficult and eventually the villagers living in between mountains see me walking towards the other mountain. "Why are you doing this?" they say. "Why would you ever leave your mountain?" I continue, ignoring the people, my eyes focused on the mountain so far in the distance that I can no longer see it from the ground. The path becomes more desolate, the village is far behind, only dust and sand lie ahead. I am dirty, tired, thirsty, and hopeless. So I fall. My face down, weeping into the sand at my failure. Little did I know the one who I was looking for stands right before me, waiting for me to look up.

"I'm sorry." The only true words that I have said to Him in a while. He picks me up and puts me on my feet.

"I never doubted you," He says.

Then the real tears came. I was sitting in the second seat from the end of the row in a hall, my eyes still closed in the palms of my hands, tear drops streaming down my face in silent prayer. I never thought that I could stand up in that desert. I've been on that desert floor for so long I never thought that I could possibly continue on, searching for that other mountain. I had convinced myself that I was making that trek alone.

That was the first time in months that I stayed focused during prayer for that long. I didn't open my eyes until the speaker was done walking us through that image. The hurt that ran through my body slowly dissipated—it was still there—but for the first time instead of hesitating to take that leap, instead of putting that wall of insecurity between me and God, I opened my heart just enough for the light to peek through the crack.

The one thing about keeping the faith is that sometimes it slips right through your fingers. I am impatient, and I love to have things my way as fast as I possibly can. I love to be in the know at all times. I love to have control over all aspects in my life;

it's why I hate group projects, since I don't know what other people are going to say and if they will say it right. I am too afraid of the unknown that I try and keep everything in my line of sight: no surprises. God has a different idea though. I can't fix myself or have it all under control before I sit down to pray.

After that session with the speaker, my heart started to open up a little more. I didn't walk through the convention center worrying about the night's prayer. I was still broken a good bit; these things take time, no matter how much I want to fast pass my way through them.

The day passed into night; groups from different parishes throughout the country crowded the streets, still rainy, chanting for their home state and trying to find a place to eat that wasn't already packed with people. We were only a group of four, allowing us to slip into restaurants with hardly a wait. We went to Primanti Brothers, the place famous for their sandwiches stacked with tons of meat and fries. I was already filled with fried foods from lunch earlier and then dinner the night before. My body couldn't take a sandwich larger than my face, not to mention the ghost of my mother's words to not eat garbage the whole trip rang in my ears. I got a salad, even though my mouth watered at the idea of the famous sandwich. Eventually we made our way to Lucas Oil stadium, a crowd of teenagers already there, waiting to get inside for the night's concert and session.

I could go on and on about the concert and the session that night. Matt Maher was performing, one of the most famous Christian singers today, and my personal favorite. AJ and I were determined to get front row to see him (we did) and to get on the floor of the stadium for Adoration (we did that, too). It was a lot of fun, and I won't forget it. But, despite the great talents of Matt Maher and the great spot we had for Adoration, it still wasn't the highlight of the National Catholic Youth Conference, at least for me.

The next day was our last day at the conference. We went to talks from different speakers and toured the hall where all the booths were set up. We had a nice dinner, and then we went back to Lucas Oil stadium, not rushing as much this time, but still wanting to get a good seat; the procession for the Mass was supposedly really cool, and we wanted a good view.

We got into the stadium and found four open seats in front of a group from the Archdiocese of Indianapolis, right behind where all the priests sat. We were going to have Mass that night, in a stadium full of 25,000 people. It's the largest Mass I've ever been to and probably will ever be at in my life. I was fearful. That fear I felt at the smaller, daily Mass yesterday came back. If I couldn't focus then, how could I focus now? I still wasn't fixed completely, and although Jesus picked me up in the desert, I forced myself to think that I fell right back down and this time there was no getting up.

Mass began. There was a beautiful procession of priests and bishops pouring in from the entrance to left of where we sat. It seemed like they were never ending, a whole sea of little red caps marching out and bowing, only to let the priests enter, all dressed in cream. The procession took longer than the opening prayer. The bishop of Los Angeles was the one performing the Mass. He had a soft voice, and an accent from somewhere in Latin America. It was like any other Mass in form, the readings, and the prayers, and the homily were all structured the same. But then came the time for holy Communion. The section full of priests filed into a line to distribute the Eucharist to thousands of people. My fear was increasing, and my heart was heavy with the realization that I had to see God face to face, and I was still not fixed. How could I be worthy of receiving the Eucharist? To take Jesus, most high and most holy, into my body unclean and broken? It didn't feel right, even though I had received absolution of my sins just twenty-four hours before. Regardless, I stayed kneeling, pleading with God, my eyes clenched shut, hoping that I could see what He wanted me to see.

My section must've been one of the last ones to have a priest distributing the Eucharist. We were in the first row, so we got up, our knees sore and numb from kneeling on hard ground and followed in a line to the priest. The line shortened, and then the priest was right in front of me, holding the Eucharist in front of my face.

"The Body of Christ," he said.

"Amen," and I opened my mouth, leaning my head up towards the priest. He placed the Eucharist on my tongue and I walked back to my seat and kneeled again.

I was tired, not just physically, but spiritually. I had worked myself into believing that something was so wrong with me, only I could fix it. I was tired of the constant stress I put on myself to be perfect around others. To not falter in any way so people wouldn't think bad of me, and then in turn think bad of my religion, and then think bad of God. I was tired of being tired. My soul just simply couldn't take any more beatings from the brain. I sat there on my knees, my arms in front of my body, my eyes closed, and my mouth shut, but everything inside me was just saying let go.

Somehow, my mind started to release its death grip on doubt. I knew that I couldn't go on any more thinking so terribly of myself that I wouldn't even let my Creator into my heart. There was no longer room for hesitation.

It may sound strange, but a lot of times when I pray, I can feel my heart beating. I hear it pumping blood to the rest of my body, and I feel the rhythmic thumps inside my chest. I take it as a sign from the Holy Spirit, letting me know that I am alive, and that I am His. I felt my heart beating on the floor of that stadium during Mass. I moved my hands from in front of my torso to be crossed over my heart, wanting to feel that love closer. Once I moved my hands up, a thought crossed my head.

"I am woman. I am beautiful."

I felt a type of joyous confusion. I was explaining my brokenness to God and then this of all things graces my thoughts. I found myself talking to Jesus, this time though, He didn't feel distant. I felt him within the depths of my chest, and in the beating of my heart. *You really think I'm beautiful*, I thought. I couldn't help but feel surprised. The whole time I felt unworthy. I was dumbfounded by the simple, yet profound message sent to me that day in the form of my thoughts, something that was plaguing me over the past few months before the trip. At first, I couldn't understand why this was what God wanted me to hear. I wasn't concerned about not being beautiful or not being woman enough. But like He does, He worked on my heart, showing me all the things that he has meant for me to understand for a long time.

Over the past few months, so many feelings were jumbled in my mind that I didn't know what to do with them. The truth was I felt overwhelmingly ugly on the inside. I felt like I wasn't being the "right me." That night at Mass was the first time in a long time I felt truly beautiful. I didn't care about what anyone was going to say about me. I was myself that night, a beautiful woman, holding onto Jesus within the depths of her heart, never letting go.

When Mass ended, the band played one more song before we had to leave. Everyone in the stadium was dancing and so was I. I danced with all the love I had in my body (which was a lot) not letting those grimy thoughts back into my brain. When we finally left the stadium, we got back on our bus along with fifty others from the Archdiocese of Baltimore and we drove straight home. I didn't sleep much because that bus was terribly uncomfortable. But when I woke up that morning I felt a different type of rest. A calmness I can't describe.

14. Papaw

On the day after Halloween in sixth grade, I walked up to my language arts teacher's desk, elevated from the rest of the classroom by about two steps, and told her that I was going to miss class since I had to go to Johnstown for my grandpa's funeral. She was young and newly married—her name had changed the year before she was my teacher. When I told her, she gave me the sympathetic look that all ladies give you when you tell them sad news. Their shoulders go down and their eyes seem to fill with concern, and their lips form a tiny tight smile, and they tilt their head. She held out her arms to give me a hug and rolled closer to me in her teacher-chair. She squeezed me tight and told me that she was sorry.

I told all my other teachers, but she was the first one since she taught my favorite class—language arts—so she was my favorite teacher.

I had found out that my Papaw (as me and my sister called him—my cousins would tend to call him Pop Pop, but that was already the name of my other grandfather, so he needed a different one), had passed away the afternoon of Halloween, after school, but before we went trick-or-treating. My parents had found out that morning but had waited to tell Olivia and me, so we could enjoy our day at school. Halloween was my favorite school day of the year. Everybody wore their costumes to school; I looked forward to this in anticipation, waiting to show off my carefully picked Party City costume to all my friends, waiting for them to tell me how good it looked.

Before he passed away, Papaw was going into surgery for something to do with his arteries. He had a history of some heart problems. Before I was born he had a triple bypass, something I never understood, but knew that it was a big deal, since whenever my parents talked about him and told other people about the surgery their eyes widened and their necks stuck out a little. They would mutter a "Wow" or "Really?" after hearing about it. When Papaw went in for his surgery, I was told it was a simple one, and it was. Compared to the severity of a triple bypass, this one was easy as pie.

Despite this, it didn't stop my incessant worrying. In middle school I was a serious worry wart, as my mom called it. I worried about everything and worried about it too much. Most of it stemmed from an intense germaphobia that I developed when I was in elementary school after I came down with a terrible and unforgiving stomach bug. After that, I was determined never to come in contact with a germ again. Since then I worried constantly about getting sick. I would go to the bathroom twice in each class just to wash my hands. At night, when I said my prayers, I would ask God to keep my whole family from getting any type of sickness or feeling any type of symptom. I would get into the specifics, just so He would understand.

My worrying about germs spread to worry about others too. I hated when my parents went out for a date by themselves, or if my mom left home one day to go grocery shopping. I would always stay up way past my bedtime until they came home, just to see them open the door myself—I couldn't sleep otherwise. I would debate for an hour whether or not to call them while they were out; I didn't want to bother them, but at the same time, I wanted to make sure that they were okay.

When looking at my history of intense concern and fretting about everything, it only made sense that I worried about Papaw's surgery. I would talk to my dad about his surgery and if he would be okay, knowing every time he would say everything would be fine, and to remember to say a prayer for him. So that's what I did.

The day I came home from school, my mom told me that the surgery went well, and that Papaw was fine. In any other circumstance, finding out that the surgery went well would subside my worries, like seeing my parents walk into the living room after a night out, but this time the worries lingered in a sort of watered down way.

When my dad came home from work one day, he told me that the hospital was keeping Papaw there to keep an eye on his vitals. He didn't seem worried, so I tried hard to suppress my concern for my grandfather. I didn't know what vitals meant, but the word sounded serious, and even when my dad explained it to me, the worry was still there just as strong. Call it intuition, or just a feeling, but despite my family's efforts to comfort me, I wasn't about to let go of worry until my grandfather was back at his home.

My dad called Papaw on the phone that day, to check up on him after the surgery. I was in the living room when he dialed the number. Dad walked past the couch I was sitting on when he answered the phone, on his way to the stairs. His voice always got louder when he talked on the phone, regardless of who he was talking too. He felt the need to project his voice as if the receiver on the other side filtered out all the sound. He made a joke about Papaw making friends with the nurses, and them wanting him to stay.

I can't remember if I talked to Papaw on that same phone call, or if my Mom called him later for me to say hello to him. All I remember is taking the phone from my mom and hearing his slight scratchy voice through the telephone. I can't remember what our conversation was about. Here's what I do remember: It was short. I didn't know exactly what to say. I asked him how he was doing, even though I knew he would say he was doing alright. When the conversation was coming to a close I walked over to my mom or dad, laying on the couch to hand over the phone.

"I love you," I told Papaw. I always made a habit of saying I love you before I hung up the phone or before I left someplace. It was a side effect of my being a worry wart. I always wanted to make sure that the person I was leaving knew that I loved them just in case I would never see them again. It's a morbid thought for an eleven-year-old, but it was a precaution I would never forget to take.

"I love you too, honey," he said. For a long time, I was kicking myself for forgetting if he said, "I love you too, honey," or "I love you too, sweetheart." I was writing a poem about him and I completely forgot the last word he said to me. One time I mentioned to my mom that I was mad at myself for not remembering the words that Papaw said to me before he passed. She told me he would have said "honey" not "sweetheart." But knowing Papaw's last words to me didn't diminish the anger I held against myself, since I knew that I didn't even know my grandfather enough to know his term of endearment for me.

My dad left a day later to go visit him in Johnstown. Both his brothers went too. It was rare that my dad went to visit his parents without us, but my sister and I couldn't miss school.

On Halloween morning I noticed nothing different about my mom. My dad had already left for work early in the morning. Every morning I heard Dad get up and walk past my room and down the steps. Sometimes he worked out in the basement before work and I heard the clanking of the weights all the way from the third floor. That morning was the same as all the rest. I went out to the bus stop, anxious to get to school on one of the most exciting days of the year. Whenever I was excited I got over-energetic and I could not stop talking. It was like all my energy built up and would come out in uncontrolled spurts. This was how it always was on days like this at school, the days where all the teachers ditch their lesson plans for some game or activity that has to do with the holiday.

That day passed like every other Halloween school day. I can't remember my costume or what we did in class that day; I was too focused on getting home and going trick-or-treating. When I got off the bus that day, I went home through the garage. That day in my memory skips a little like an old scratchy CD. The next moment is me sitting on the golden couch in our living room. The TV, my favorite source of background noise, was off so it was extra quiet. I sat curled up against my dad who was behind me, and I was facing my sister and my mother. My parents told me the bad news, as they called it. My mom's face was red, and all her features were downturned; her eyes, her mouth, and her seemingly everything else. When they told me, I said "What?" My voice high pitched and loud like it always is when I'm upset. I don't know why I said "What" since I knew what they were going to say. We've never had news bad enough where they had to sit us down on the couch as a family. My sister just started crying, no build-up or sniffling, tears sprung right away, her face turned down in an expression of immense upset.

At this point, the only one not crying was my dad. It was his father who died, but I knew he wouldn't cry, since he never did. I only ever saw him cry once. It was when I was very little. I was on the couch looking over into the kitchen. My dad and mom were in the center of my vision, standing in front of the stove. My dad leaned his head on my mom's shoulder and he cried. I remember asking mom why dad was crying, and she said "He was stressed at work." Whether this answer was true or not, I don't know. There are times when I think about this moment and I question if it really happened. My memory isn't perfect, and it was so long ago that it was possible I could have dreamt it. I doubt it, since it felt real, and my imagination had a habit of creating wild and fantastical dreams while I was asleep—and this was right in the kitchen.

I went up to my room shortly after they told me the news. I sat on my bed and just thought. I zone out a lot, staring into space, and letting my mind wander away from wherever I was. My cousins and friends used to make fun of me for it, since I would zone out multiple times while we were together in the middle of a conversation. I was alone though, this time. After finding out my grandfather had passed, I wanted to know how to react. How exactly I should respond. I tried to make it make sense. I tossed around thoughts in my head, bouncing them back and forth from side to side in my skull. I was trying to make myself feel that Papaw was no longer with us. I knew I would never see him again, but that's different than truly feeling the weight of the change. That's the whole idea of letting it "sink in" we talk about when something drastic happens, good or bad. The idea is too big for our human brains, and even though we know as a fact something just took place, feeling the effects of it right away doesn't hit us at the moment we know it. It comes in douses of pain resonating throughout time, in different places, and points in life.

I'm grateful that I wasn't able to make sense of my grandfather's death that day; the burden of feeling it all at once would simply weigh too much and my heart would bend like a bridge under pressure. I sat staring at nothing, hoping God would come out of that nothingness and snap me out of it. For the first time I let myself zone out because I was alone and there was no one to mock me for it, but more so because it was more comfortable than being present.

Even though my Papaw had just died that morning, Halloween was still happening. I got back in my costume as soon as possible and went outside where the neighbors gathered around a few tables that held chicken nuggets for the neighborhood kids to eat. I went outside excited to see the other kids and go trick-or-treating with other neighbors. The thought of my grandfather faded for a moment, replaced by the left-over energy from the school day for the holiday.

There were two feelings that dominated that night: guilt and bitterness. I had shoved the pain of my grandfather dying down deep so I could enjoy Halloween night as a child. And I did. After I went to sleep that night, thoughts about how I should act permeated my brain, preventing my sleep: *How dare I enjoy myself during such a grievous time in my family? Am I a fake for not being sad just hours after hearing the news?* Thoughts like these turned my brain over and tousled it like it was in a spin cycle for days. *How should I act and feel and be?*

The second—bitterness—entered when I first interacted with others after hearing about the death. Some neighbors already knew about my grandfather passing. One of the neighbor's daughters came up to me and said, "I'm sorry about your grandfather." I responded with "It's okay. Thank you," But my thoughts differed greatly. My mind went straight to the cynical: *Her mom probably told her to say that, and she doesn't even mean it.* Before that night, my naïve eleven-year-old heart believed the best of people, always finding ways to justify bad behavior or destructive decisions, hoping their heart was in the right place but their mind just didn't cooperate. But my own heart wasn't in the right place— it was cluttered with too many emotions for a young girl to handle. The struggle of losing a grandparent is different than the loss of someone in the immediate family. My grandfather was someone significant in my life, but not as often present as my parents or sister. I couldn't find where to fall on the scale of grief: I felt guilty for expressing my great sadness, for those who lose a parent experience a greater loss, and I felt guilty for not being sad enough since my grandfather deserved to be mourned over. This limbo stage of emotion impacted my vision of others and casting a murky shadow over the way I saw others' intentions.

The bitterness I developed that night was like my internal expression slowly deteriorating to a scowl, while my external expression focused on the happy thought of getting free candy and staying up later than usual.

My spin cycle of emotions in my head weren't helped when I went to school the next day, when I told my best friend at the time that my grandfather had died. I don't know how I expected her to react, but what she said stuck me with a searing shot of pain—deepening my confusion.

To put what she said into context, the year before middle

school began there was a boy named Dustin whose father passed away in the middle of the school year.

I walked up the metal steps to the bus and sat in one of the first four rows of seats; our bus followed the age old oldest-in-the-back-youngest-in-the-front-rule, so us sixth graders were confined to the first few seats. I was the last stop on the bus, so my best friend Claire, was already sitting on the outside edge on one of the seats. I took the one across from her.

"My grandfather died," I told her rather abruptly, not wanting to waste time telling someone. I wanted someone other than my parents to comfort me, since they were experiencing grief themselves. I wanted someone unaffected to help me out in some way.

"Well, how do you think Dustin felt?" That was her response. She gave me a look as if to express that what she was saying was obvious. She turned forward in her seat, away from me, and I turned back in, not knowing what to do or say—letting that spin cycle toss more guilt into my brain.

We had to leave after a few days, so we could be with my Nana, what we called my grandmother, and prepare for the viewing and funeral, hence why I told my teachers I would miss school. We got to Johnstown, a three-and-a-half-hour drive away and we stayed with my grandmother, who, like Dad, I didn't see cry. There was all kinds of food and flowers cluttering the kitchen and tables. So many people had brought my grandmother these things to send their condolences and none of us knew what to do with all of it.

Then there was the viewing. We had a small personal service in the funeral home with just our family and without all the others who wanted to pay their respects. Our whole family sat in rows of chairs in front of the open casket, while someone I didn't know said some words about "John," which was Papaw's real first name. I sat in the second row. My dad, his two brothers, and my grandmother sat in the front. After the man stopped talking and we were left in silence, I saw one of my uncles turn towards my aunt and cry. I had never seen him cry either; in fact, I had never seen a grown man in my family cry. I thought they were invincible, not letting anything phase them. In that moment, I saw the humanity that resonated through every person in that room, the loss of a father, all through the tears of my poor uncle.

We all went up to Papaw after that, or maybe it was after the viewing. I can't remember much of a timeline, only the spurts of emotion, so everything is out of order, fixing itself in degrees of grief in my brain. I went up to Papaw at the casket. This was the first time I had seen a dead person before, and it was my grandfather. He didn't look like Papaw anymore, not even John. He looked too perfect, his face too pale and his expression too complacent. I saw some people kiss him on the forehead when they went to see him, but I was too scared and thought people might judge me, so I kissed my hand and placed it on his before I walked away.

The pallbearers were my dad, uncles, my one male cousin, and there must've been two other men who I can't remember since there are usually six.

The funeral was at St. Benedict's Church, the church that my dad and his brothers had gone to as children. It was where Nana and Papaw were in the choir. The church was slightly smaller in size than my home parish at St. Joseph. There were only about four sections of rows, two large ones with rows extending to the back of the church, and two smaller ones on the outer edge that only extended halfway down the church before the exit doors stopped them. There were stained glass windows on either side, filtering colored light through the pews. Sometimes when it was sunny on a Sunday that we visited, the light would be so strong you could see the rays in sharp lines coming through the windows, almost like the childish drawings of the sun. I can't remember if it was sunny that day. We sat in the first row since we were the family. The priest presiding over the funeral Mass was Father Pallis, the pastor of St. Benedicts. His voice was smooth and the perfect pitch. Every word he spoke made me feel like I was the only one he was talking to. When he spoke I heard more than his voice—a glimmer of something else that made you feel at home. After that, he became my favorite priest. I couldn't wait to go back to Johnstown to visit my grandmother and attend Mass, since I knew I would hear his homilies.

Later in the Mass, one of Papaw's friends sang *Ave Maria*. It was beautiful, and a real tear jerker if the event itself wasn't tear jerker enough. After the Mass, we talked to the lady who sang the song, who was also a part of the choir with Papaw and complimented her voice.

"Thank you. Yeah, John came up to me one day and

said, 'Barb, I want you to sing *Ave Maria* at my funeral.' I said sure, but you might have to sing it at mine!" she said, causing a fit of giggles from all of us. We saw her occasionally at church when we visited. Sometimes I still ask my dad about how she's doing, since she so beautifully granted my Papaw's request

After the funeral, we had a lunch for all the guests at the funeral at a place nearby called Anthony's. I had only been there twice in my entire life, both were after funerals. While everybody was eating, guests told their stories about Papaw, most of them were funny, causing the whole room to erupt with laughter from the memory of my grandfather. I wanted to go up and tell a story, so I asked my dad to go up and tell it for me, but he said I could go and do it myself. But I chickened out.

I wanted to tell the story of when both my Nana and Papaw came down to stay with us for a week in Maryland while my parents went to the Grand Canyon for their anniversary. At this time, my favorite card game was Texas Hold 'em, a form of poker I had learned at camp weekend. I loved playing it with anybody who knew how, and as a child in elementary school, not many of my peers could play poker without me explaining the rules tediously, multiple times. Luckily my grandparents knew how to play, so my sister, Nana, Papaw, and I got together in the living room one night they were visiting and played the game. Both my grandparents sat on the couch, while my sister and I sat on the floor, hiding our hands from each other. One time my grandfather made a bold bet with a straight face. All of us were shocked at the amount of plastic coins he tossed in the pile. I thought his hand was a whole lot of nothing—and that he was bluffing, the official term for betting more than your hand is worth. Apparently, my grandma thought so too, exclaiming, "Oh, that Papaw is buffaloing!" I busted out laughing so hard—the kind where sound doesn't even come out and you just look like a fool with your mouth open and your head shaking. Everyone was laughing, but I'm pretty sure I was the most hysterical—the mess up of the word was the height of comedy at that point and I could barely keep a straight face the rest of the game. To this day, I still chuckle at the memory, my grandma calling out Papaw with such confidence, only to have us laugh at her mistake for days after.

My grandma's blunder now feels insignificant. If I imagine the situation without myself in it, it looks like a poorly executed joke on a sitcom. But for years it was my favorite story to tell. I would even explain the whole game of Texas Hold 'Em to my friends so they would understand the full hilarity of what she said. Regardless, I still didn't share the story at Anthony's. I was afraid nobody would laugh the same way I did, and I wasn't ready to hand over that moment to others. That moment with my grandparents is something that is purely mine. All other times in my life I was with them I was surrounded by my parents, cousins, uncles, and aunts and all memories were shared, which is a lovely thing, since it makes for great conversations and ensures the moments with Papaw are never forgotten. But something about sitting on the carpet in my living room, my legs crossed, hoping for a good card to flip over so I could show off my poker skills to my grandfather, the entirety of that moment with them and my sister—no matter how silly it may seem—stuck indefinitely to my brain, separately from all other memories. That was the time when they were *my* grandparents.

Sixth grade that year, in language arts class, we had a unit on imagery. I felt I was good at describing things and I read a lot so it only made sense that I would flourish in that unit. The first task, a sort of pretest on our knowledge of imagery, was to write about a big event in our lives, one where we felt overly happy, or overly sad. Then we would give that description to a partner, and they would draw it out and show it to the class to see how well it matched the event. The girl I partnered with was a close friend of mine. I think the event she chose to write about was finding out they were going to Disney World, or something else really exciting. I chose to write about learning my grandfather had died. There were other big events in my life, happy ones, but that was the most recent and fresh in my mind, and I sought attention and sympathy after being so overlooked by my best friend earlier that year.

Confident that my writing was top notch and my friend had taken the picture straight from my mind and put it on the paper, we decided to go first. Of course, there were tons of things wrong—you can't expect much from a budding writer. My imagery would hopefully improve in the subsequent years. After we were finished presenting our drawings of the other's writing, we walked back to our seats, and on the way back, my teacher stopped me.

"Hey, Lauren, it's okay to write about those things."

Those were her exact words. I don't remember many conversations word for word, only a basic outline and idea, but this one I know. I nodded, saying nothing, and continued to my seat.

For many nights in the year following the death of my grandfather, I would talk to him. After I got ready for bed and covered myself with blankets, I would speak to my grandfather as if he were right there in the room with me. With my head down on the pillow, my eyes open, I would tell him about my day, what I did, and update him on the status of my mom, dad, sister, and sometimes cousins if I had seen them recently. Many times I would talk to him after an argument with my mom. Whenever I didn't get my way, I resorted to dramatic means, i.e. locking myself in my bedroom and crying into my pillow like I saw princesses do in the movies. No matter how many times I tried to look pretty while crying into my pillow, I still looked a mess, my hair knotted and matted over my face, and a mix of tears and snot running down my chin.

In these moments, I got ready for bed early and without saying goodnight to my parents. I would lie in bed, relaying all my struggles to the only one who could understand me, Papaw. Me ranting about my kid struggles to my grandfather seems strange since I never complained to him when he was on Earth. But this was before I was allowed to have a phone, so texting my friends was out of the question. I didn't want to go to my sister, since she was younger than me and would perceive me as weak. So the only one I know who would listen to me was Papaw, and did I talk his ear off. I would stay up late just having a one-sided conversation with him, often in a whisper and in between tears left over from anger towards my mother. I don't know why I started talking to him, maybe it was because he was closer to God, or that I was making up for lost time.

I did stop talking to him, though. I can't remember when, but there came a time when I lived a day and wouldn't think about him. Every Halloween for the next few years I would still dress up like everyone else, but the holiday always tasted bitter since the memory of loss overpowered the excitement of going to school.

A little over six years have passed since the death of my grandfather and on each Halloween since then I acknowledge his death less and less. On Halloween morning, I used to wake up with a wave of emotion weighing on my heart from the anniversary of what took place on that day. What made that day different wasn't the costumes, trick-or-treating, jack-o-lanterns or scary movies, but the loss I was reminded of when I woke up at six o' clock, the time he had passed. But as the distance grows between his death and the present, I think of him every year less and less. And thus the guilt returns. To me, thinking about Papaw on the anniversary of his death was the least I could do to acknowledge all he has done for me, my dad, his brothers, and the Goodwin family as a whole. But, now, with the passing of time and the hustle of life, I can't even seem to do that. One year, I totally forgot about the anniversary of his death until I got home from school, hours passing of me being awake on the day God took him home and I didn't even stop to think once of him.

Another side effect of time is my memory of Papaw himself. There are times when I forget his face or voice. When I think about him, the general shape and features come through, but the distinct features seem like they have a fog over them, preventing me from distinguishing the specialness that his face really was. I can't remember what his eyes looked like when he looked at me. Or what it felt like when his tall frame would bend down to hug my small skinny one. I can't remember his smile. I know he smiled and laughed often, but the sounds and pictures don't match up in my brain.

So many memories clutter my brain in quick spurts like a montage of my life with him. Times at our family vacation in Rehoboth, when he would go back to the beach house we had rented earlier than everybody else, or sometimes he wouldn't come down at all. I would ask my mom sometimes to go back up to the beach house early too. For one, I didn't like the beach much then because I always got sand in my bathing suit and wanted to get home early so I could shower, and I didn't want Papaw to be alone on our family vacation, although I'm sure he didn't mind it; he was just like that. I didn't know why. I only knew that I wanted him to stay down there. Or one time when we stayed in the Outer Banks and I was making toast for breakfast. When it popped out of the toaster, brown and golden crispy it looked perfect, so perfect I wanted to show Papaw how good I was at making toast. I held up the toast to show him so he could see form where he was sitting in the living room, but I had already buttered it and my mom saw me holding it up, and afraid that I would drop it on the floor, she told me to put it down, and I did before Papaw got to see it.

Other memories with him take place at his and Nana's house in Johnstown. He had this huge and extremely comfortable green recliner that could fit both Olivia and I when we were little. It was so comfortable; Olivia and I would fight over who got to sit in it. I would also ask my mom every time we visited if I could sleep there. When Olivia and I arrived at their house, antsy from sitting in a car for over three hours, we ran to his big green chair and squeezed ourselves in. Every time we both sat in it, without fail, Papaw would walk over, proclaim "That's my seat!" or "Get out of my chair!" and then pretend to sit on us. My sister and I would put our feet on his back and push him off with all our might until he "fell" onto the ground. Then my dad would walk in, saying "Look what you did to your poor Papaw!"

A big part of our visits in Johnstown was going to Mass on Sundays. We went up there every year for Easter, so we would bring our Easter dresses that we picked out from Macy's or some other big store, and get all dressed up after we opened our Easter baskets in the morning for Mass. Papaw always looked so tall to me in Mass if I sat next to him. When we would kneel, my face barely came over the pew, and I had to lift up my shoulders in a perpetual shrug just to get them to the typical prayer position. Papaw, though, could lean on the pew, his torso extending well over the bench. When we would sing hymns, I remember looking up at him from where I was standing. He seemed so big, holding the hymnal in his hands, I only reaching half his height. He was the tallest person I knew.

There was one thing during Mass that I never paid attention to. I was focused on opening the hymnal, singing the songs, kneeling at the right time, saying the right things, holding his hand during the Our Father, and more, that I never made an effort to listen to him sing. That is my biggest regret. Everyone tells me how lovely a voice he had. He sang in the choir, and even went on a trip to the Vatican with the church choir to sing for Pope John Paul II—I didn't know that fact until after he died, and even if I did I wouldn't know the magnitude of it until later. I can hear Father Pallis, talking about how he gave his voice to St. Benedict's for a long time. I like to think of it as his service to the church. Yet, I still don't know what his singing sounded like. It's not a memory I forgot, because I never knew it in the first place. I specifically remember standing next to him at Mass, a hymnal in my hand and one in his, and looking up at him, seeing his mouth form the words to the song, but letting the collective voices of the people drown out his own. I wish I had listened closer, heard his voice sing so faithfully to God and tucked it in a special place in my memory so I could take it out in times of struggle. That way he would be here with me. I wish I could have heard him sing *Ave Maria*, just to me, so that every time I went into church and opened a hymnal Papaw's sweet voice would sing to me from Heaven.

15. Camping Memoir #4

Our new camp destination was a rented cabin. We hadn't rented anything for camp besides the one year after the trailer was sold. It was hardly what you would call camping. When most people think of camping, they think of putting up tents in the woods, sleeping in sleeping bags and peeing behind some trees. Our new cabin had a kitchen nicer than my house and a hot tub. We almost felt bad that we had such luxurious accommodations when we were supposed to be living in nature for a weekend, but after we got into the hot tub, we didn't regret it at all.

There were fewer of us than last year or years before. But the girls who had been going over ten years still came. My cousin even drove four hours from college just to visit for one night. All of us still hung out together, playing card games, corn hole, and more. We still cooked all our meals on the fire (except the Saturday breakfast of course). We didn't have our beloved places like the covered bridge or the dirt hill, so we decided to do something new and go white water rafting at the nearby Youghiogheny river. This idea caused my mother extreme worry, as she knew white water rafting could easily get dangerous. We left with the constant demand to wear helmets ingrained in our minds—my mom repeated it so many times there was no way we could forget.

Our camp weekend came after a week-long downpour, which meant the river water was high and fast-moving. We were only supposed to go on a shorter course through the rapids, which would normally take two hours, but because of all the rain, it would only take fifteen minutes. To get our money's worth, we took the full course through the rapids, which was about an hour and a half (it was supposed to take four). We split up our rafts, so my family, including my cousins and my uncle were in one, and everyone else was in another. As we went down the river we yelled and taunted one another, so much so our river guide had to really make sure we would row to get through the water. My cousins and I made our fathers sit in the front, so we wouldn't get the worst of the waves, and although they were thoroughly soaked by the end, it didn't matter, because so were we. Only one person fell out of our raft the whole trip, which is pretty good, especially because it wasn't me. We were going through a series of large waves when the raft catapulted my cousin Kelsey up and into the water. We swiftly puller her in with no damage.

After the trip was over, our camp group lingered around the white-water rafting place waiting for some of the girls who decided to change so they wouldn't stick to the seats on the way back. We continued talking to the river guides who navigated us through the water. They were a great group of people, and I'm pretty sure only two of the guys had hair shorter than his shoulders, and one of whom had his hair shaved into a Mohawk.

We were standing by the trunk of my uncle's car, snacking on some food we brought when one of the river guides walked over and said, "I heard there were cheese balls." We brought a huge plastic container filled with cheese balls, which would have been more than enough for us and the river guides, if we hadn't left the container outside with the lid off to be rained on later that night. (No one wants a soggy cheese ball.)

We made our way back to camp after thanking the river guides, exhausted from the day's trip. We couldn't wait to get home and cook mountain pies. Not only were we starving, but we were ready to get into the hot tub that awaited us. (It's pathetic how glamorous our camping was.) That Saturday night was a lot calmer than camp weekends in the past. The dads didn't play poker. Instead we all climbed in the hot tub, the warm water fizzling and bubbling as we lowered ourselves in. I only stayed in for a few minutes, wanting to get out, dry off, and change into fresh clothes. We never took showers at camp, so changing clothes was the closest we got to feeling refreshed. (The first shower when we arrived home, though, was always lovely.), I don't know why we continued this "rule." Some people broke it, but most of us stayed true to our tradition, even though the last two places we stayed at for camp had fully functioning showers.

We still brought our music with us. We didn't have the big speaker anymore to stand in the patio, but we did have a smaller one to connect with an iPhone. We all fought over who would be the DJ and choose the music to play. No one wanted to do it and face the scrutiny if they didn't play any good songs. The safe option was *Take Me Home, Country Roads*. It was a crowd pleaser. Odds are, once it was over someone would say "again!" and we'd break out into song once more (Even though we weren't in West Virginia anymore).

I remember sitting around the campfire that evening, watching the sun go down before me. During camp weekend, I was always aware of the oncoming darkness. In early years, I had an intense fear of the dark, and always paid attention to how fast the evening turned into nighttime so I could whip out my flashlight when need be. Sitting around the campfire that night, I paid attention to how fast the sun was going down like I did before. Except, I wasn't running around with the other girls like I did previous years, using my flashlight to guide my way. I was enjoying the fire a soda in my hand, watching the sparks fly up from the firewood. I felt a calmness I had never felt before from camp. Camp was always exciting, rowdy, chaotic, and different. I didn't feel that this Saturday. Camp was still rowdy and exciting, but more mellow than in years past. Camp weekend wasn't the same as it always used to be when I was little. But it was still *camp*. Camp: a word that is its own adjective for those who attend it. Simply saying camp evokes memories made and stories told every year. It exudes the very excitement of arriving at a campfire already burning with the people you haven't seen since last year sitting around it. I was worried after that Saturday that camp was changing, moving away from my grasp; but it wasn't. Camp was growing with me and every other daughter, son, and dad who went.

For me, camp has been a constant. I could always count on it to take me out of whatever world I was living in, one full of stress, pressures, and worry. I could go to camp and simply have fun—what a kid needs. At my next camp I won't be a kid anymore, but I don't think it will matter since there are now more adults who attend than kids. Camp isn't something you grow out of. And so it continues. I don't know for how long. I hope forever. Life may carry us in different directions, down different paths with twists and turns we will need to deal with on our own. I think we all need that weekend, to take us off life's path for just a moment.

16. The Greatest Love

"You formed my inmost being;
You knit me in my mother's womb
I praise you, because I am wonderfully
made;
wonderful are your works!"
Psalm 139: 13-14

I wish I could say I came out of the womb praising God for my new life and counting rosary beads on my tiny fingers. I wish following the Lord came as easy as learning to tie my shoes. I want to say my relationship with God is in tip-top shape. I can't say that, but I do know He always holds up His end of the bargain. To be loved by God is easy, to accept that love is hard, and to love Him is even harder. It simply makes sense to love God, but we humans tend to screw things up. God created the entire universe in its vastness and mystery. He sculpted the shores of the ocean and the softness of the sand. He created us individually with the same love, care, and intentionality with which he made the highest mountains. How could we not love a being so giving of Himself to us, especially after He sacrificed the life of an only Son for our sake?

God is abstract. Our earthly adjectives can't even begin to describe His greatness. I think this is one of the reasons why we find it so hard to love Him. Knowing is something so deeply ingrained in all our minds. To know is to have power; to be smart; to be loved and admired. With God, we just can't know it all; at least, not while we're here on this Earth. And it's scary to think about. It's why growing up is so hard to comprehend—we don't know what is ahead, and if we choose to follow God, it's like choosing to follow something we can't completely understand. It seems foolish in the eyes of society. Whenever we make a bold decision, someone makes sure to ask us, "Do you know what you're getting into?"

When following God, I don't know. But that's the point. Trying to navigate through life with its messy and ugly turns by ourselves is impossible. Especially when we may not have even discovered our purpose or figured out what we want to do with our lives. God knows, though. I have no idea what I am going to get myself into, but I am trusting the Lord of all creation, the being who created my entire self intricately, weaving my existence together for a purpose. I am trying to give my life over to Him. He knows it better. My life was His to begin with. He knows what is right for me

17. Mom Mom's

On a bright autumn afternoon, my Dad drives on the semi-desolate Route 439, winding through farms and fields, past cows and horses wandering about the landscape. At the top of a hill we wait, the blinker clicking, to turn into the driveway that leads to the house of my maternal grandparents. The high-pitched clicks of the golden Honda minivan jump start my heart; it was the sound letting me know we were close. We are right below the apex of the hill when we turn into the driveway, so we couldn't see any oncoming cars until they were right next to us. My dad would turn down the music and open the window to listen to them, and when it was clear, he would whip the car around into the driveway. The driveway wraps around the house and takes us to the back door, even though I thought it was the front door since it's always the one I went through. Behind the house, the driveway extends up to the garage, but you couldn't tell since tractors and mowers were cluttered across the whole thing, spilling into the yard surrounding it. It is where my grandfather continues to work well into his eighties, fixing tractors and cars for locals.

My grandmother meets me at the door. Mom Mom, we call her. She is small in stature, not reaching five feet, her hair short and curled, darker than my mother's. She greets us in her Irish accent, watered down from years in America. She walks us into the small kitchen where my grandfather greets us from the table, his chair right by the phone on the wall, attached to a long curly cord, probably so he can answer whenever the phone rings in case it's someone that needs him. He always answers the phone with "Yellow" in his rough voice. Really it sounds like "Yella," a strange and far-off deviation of hello.

. . .

When I see my grandmother, I can't help but think of the steps she took, carrying her from Ireland to America. I imagine her stepping on a plane for the first time, knowing it was taking her to a place where everything was unknown, and that it wouldn't take her back home. She was going to work for a family in Florida as a live-in maid to help support her own family in Ireland. I wonder what it was like for her to know so little of where she was going to be—she was only given an alarm clock set to 6:30, to leave on time for her flight and a menu of what to cook for dinner the night she arrived in the United States.

. . .

The lot that my grandparents lived on felt like the farmland in movies. The field of corn that expanded behind their house reminded me of the hills Maria ran on in the *Sound of Music*. It's not nearly as large and clear, or even hilly as the actual landscape of Austria, but that's how it felt to me on our day trips up when I was little. They didn't live in a neighborhood. They only had a few neighbors, and all of them, except for the house across

159

the street, were relatives. Their next-door neighbor was my grandfather's sister and her husband. Down the road was my great aunt's daughter, and around the corner were the houses of her two brothers. To anyone else, it may have been the middle of nowhere, but it wasn't for me since everyone I needed was there.

Inside, we sit around the table in the kitchen while my grandmother finishes up making lunch, refusing to take a seat and rest like we tell her. Olivia and I fight over who gets to sit on the red plaid stool that's almost as tall as us. I win and climb up on the stool. It's too high; I have to lean down to eat the food my grandmother prepared. My grandfather stays in his seat, eating and drinking "Pop Pop's juice" as he calls it from a mason jar—we could never have it—I'm pretty sure it's bourbon or scotch. Mom Mom made typical comfort food: sandwiches, pasta salad, potatoes, and more. If it was a special occasion like Easter or Christmas, she'd make oyster dressing, my dad's favorite dish, and something I never ate until well into my teens.

. . .

I get my height from my grandmother. Both her and my mom stand below five feet, so when I reached 5'1" I cheered, because I never thought I would make it there. My mom always told me good things come in small packages, something a lot of petite girls probably hear. I believe it to be true since my grandmother lead by example. She is a spitfire, too. She asked me one day if I had a boyfriend, and when I told her no, she leaned in towards me and said "Shame on you!" My favorite story of my grandmother is her interaction with President John F. Kennedy, whom she met at work in the United States. Mom Mom worked for Earl T. Smith, who was the former ambassador from America to Cuba. Since he knew President Kennedy, he would often have him and his family over for dinner. When Mom Mom was serving them dinner, President Kennedy asked her, "Don't you want my autograph?" to which my grandmother responded, "If you want to give it to me."

. . .

Eventually Annette would get there. She is Mom's sister, which would make her my aunt even though she doesn't seem like it. I still wonder if Mom and Annette are actually related; they seem to be different in every possible way. My mom is quiet and reserved—the only curse word you'll hear from her is in the car when there's an idiot driver in front of her. Annette is loud and doesn't like to limit her vocabulary just because others are around. She wears hats indoors, which irritates my Mom, and loves everything hunting. She is an expert shooter, winning women's skeet competitions across Maryland. The basement of my grandparent's house has a shelf with all her glass trophies that she won. I didn't know what they signified, but I wanted them. Sometimes she would let us have them and I would put them on the shelves above my desk along with soccer team participation trophies and ribbons from gymnastics.

We never call Annette "Aunt Annette" because she doesn't feel like an aunt to us. For the better part of our lives Annette wasn't married and didn't have any kids. She spoiled us like her own. She wasn't like another parent; she didn't care about the rules like my mom. She wasn't like an older sister. Sisters fight, and we never fought, and she was thirty years older than me, and she wasn't like an aunt who you see only on the holidays and not talk to for another few months. She is a cross between all three and more.

Whenever she would visit us at home or at Mom Mom's house, she would whistle a little tune to let us know she was here. It was like the clicking of the blinker that would let us know we had arrived. Every time I heard it, Olivia and I would jump up and see her peeking around the corner, attacking her with hugs and laughter.

After our lunch we sit in the living room to watch TV. Annette would always put on a hunting show and we would complain to change it—watching two guys wearing camo sit in the middle of nowhere whispering until a deer would come into sight wasn't entertaining enough for my jumpy kid brain. Eventually we would watch "Keeping up Appearances." My grandmother would watch it all the time and I grew to enjoy laughing at Mrs. Bucket, who was determined to make everyone call her "Ms. Bouquet."

. . .

Mom Mom grew up in Donegal, Ireland, a rural area in the northern part of the country. She lived a very different life than I am living now. She grew up in a home with two other younger siblings and her parents. Her father passed away when she was young, causing her to have to grow up way faster than I did. I've never known the struggle of losing a father, nor do I want to. I can't imagine the pain of a young daughter losing the most important man in her life. Simply thinking about not having my own father with me sparks a searing pain I never want to confront at its full magnitude.

Mom Mom had to face this loss. She also had to face the struggle of growing up poor and needing to help support her family from a young age. I am still living under the roof of my parents' house. I am preparing to leave for college, and I am already living in America. I am so different from my grandmother. I am me, because of her.

. . .

After we relaxed for a while after dinner, we would beg Annette to take us out on the gator. The gator is one of the tractors that my grandfather had. It was kind of like a golf cart, but bigger, louder, faster, and green. It was our favorite part about visiting Mom Mom's. Annette would let one of us sit on her lap and drive. (We would fight over who would go first.) Once we settled on who would drive, the gator started up and took us across the yard of my great Aunt's house and into the forest behind it. There was a path made by four wheelers and other country vehicles. The trees hung over into the path, scraping our arms as we drove on the dirt path, bouncing up and down as we hit rocks, twigs, and any other natural element in our way.

Gator rides gave me adventure. Speeding through the trees and ignoring "NO TRESPASSING" signs, my hair flying around behind me while I looked out at the sun making its way toward the Earth; this is what I craved. I felt independent, grown up, like I had all the answers. There was no one else on the path to stop us, so rules didn't exist. There were no friends, only family. I could be me without judgement. I could laugh with my mouth wide open and cheer as we sped down a back road and no one would tell me I was weird or "too loud."

After driving on dirt paths, we'd make our way to a paved back road along the side of the forest. This was my favorite. The road was paved so there were no tree roots that jolted us up and down and there were no longer trees hanging down scratching at our heads. We went as fast as we could down the road. Annette would press on the pedal and we'd speed down the road stopping just before Route 439. On the left side of the road, there was a sharp drop off leading to a vast expanse of corn fields. I was always afraid if I was the one steering that I would sneeze and accidently jerk the steering wheel, causing us to tumble down the steep drop into rows of corn. Luckily it never happened.

Since we always drove the gator after dinner, the sun was always on its way down, illuminating the landscape with a beautiful orange. It was always in our eyes, and sometimes Annette would lend us her sunglasses, so we could see, but I always gave them back because they just dimmed the beauty I saw. I loved seeing the light covering all the parts of nature before me. Even though I had to squint it was still worth it.

. . .

I haven't been to Ireland yet. I want so badly to go, not only to meet my family, but to see the beauty everyone tells me is there. Everything is green, and the landscape isn't cluttered with tons of malls and shopping centers like at home. Near where my family lives stands a mountain called Mount Errigal. All of my family has climbed it and says the view from the peak is incredible.

I often wonder what it was like for my grandmother as a kid; what she did when she played with friends and siblings and what it was like to grow up in a place so beautiful.

. . .

Soon enough, we drove home, cutting through family members' yards until we got back to Mom Mom's house. When we went inside, Mom Mom would already have bowls out for ice cream. Everyone else would put black berries that we found in the forest on their ice cream, but I ate my vanilla bean plain. I was (and still am) a very picky eater and would turn my nose up at anything that looked remotely healthy.

It was around this time that my sister and I would get tired and want to go to our home back in Perry Hall. My grandparents packed up some food for us to go along with packs of organic ground beef that they got from local farms in a red cooler. We piled everything into the trunk. Sometimes before we left, my grandmother would feed the stray cats outside with cat food and leftover scraps of dinner. There were many wild cats that always came to visit my grandmother. When they had kittens, she had some twelve or thirteen cats at a time come to the little porch by the dining room for food. We sat and waited for the tiny ones to come out of the bushes and watched them lick up the water from a bowl, and then run away when we made a noise.

One time when we were packing up to head home, my mom or dad left the trunk open while we went back inside to say goodbye. I can't remember exactly who left it open—my mom will say my dad and my dad will say my mom. Regardless, after we said our goodbyes and made the forty-minute drive home, all of us were inside the house, when we heard my mom yell "Craig!" from inside the car.

"There's a cat in the car!" my mom said, her eyes wide with shock, and her voice higher from either fear or confusion. Apparently, she reached down to grab something when she felt something soft. Assuming it was one of mine or Olivia's stuffed animal, she tried to pick it up, but before she got a hold on it, the supposed stuffed animal meowed.

My dad eventually got the cat out of the car, all the while my sister and I were standing at the door connecting our house to the garage. He held the cat by its body, went to the opening of the garage, and chucked it out into the neighborhood. It landed on its feet and scurried away. That was the last time that we saw it.

The only explanation we can think of is that the cat must've hopped in our car while the trunk was open and rode with us the whole way home without us noticing. My grandmother had named the cat Fluffy, something that she doesn't normally do since the cats come and go all the time. But this one was her favorite, and unknowingly, we catnapped it and let it loose in our suburban neighborhood. There was the occasional stray cat in our neighborhood, and for a few months after that we tried to look out for Fluffy to see if it stayed in the area. There were a few times we saw a black cat, but it was never big enough to be Fluffy, and soon enough I lost hope that we could bring him back to Mom Mom.

My grandmother never held it against us that we lost her favorite cat. We would still go back up again to visit when we could. A lot of times we met for lunch on a Sunday after church. For many years the place we always met at was the Williamsburg Inn. It wasn't in Williamsburg, it was actually off Route 40, somewhere in between our houses. It was one of the only places my grandfather would agree to go to. He was very picky like me. They had good crab cakes and good cream of crab soup. (Which is my favorite soup when made right.) My grandfather knew some of the waitresses there, either from knowing them personally, or because he's been going there for years. One of our waitresses had a scratchy voice and a lot of earrings and was always joking with our family about something. I'd order a Shirley Temple, crab cakes and fries, and most of the time cream of crab soup. One of my favorite parts of dinner were the rolls. My mom would always have to stop me from eating too many, so I wouldn't spoil my dinner. But I didn't care. I could eat the whole basket and still have enough room for cream of crab.

We always met there as a family on birthdays too. We'd get a cake there, and they would write Happy Birthday and their name on it with icing. One year we went for my dad's birthday, and like usual we got a cake and they asked for his name to write on the top of it. We told them Craig, and when they brought the cake out with the candles lit, my mom noticed that on the top was written in cursive "Happy Birthday Frank." We continued to sing Happy Birthday, inserting his real name, saving that laughter until afterward. I don't know if she misheard, or maybe delivered the wrong cake to our table, but we still ate it and didn't say a word, because cake is cake, and how were they going to fix it anyway. My mom could not stop laughing on the way home from our lunch, and we called my dad Frank for a while afterwards.

After going there what felt like every other weekend for a number of years, the restaurant changed hands. We stopped going there and decided to meet at different places for our Sunday lunch. All had to meet the standards of my traditional grandfather. We tried to take him to a Hawaiian place, but he couldn't get past the fact that they didn't serve soup there.

We meet for lunch on Sundays more often than we go up to visit them now. The toll of high school sports and academics prevents us from making the hike. When we do get the chance to go up there, we go the same way, onto Route 439 past all the farmland and right below the apex of the hill. The tractors still litter the yard. My grandfather still won't retire. I haven't ridden the gator in a few years, but I'm sure it's still up there. We still laugh at Ms. Bucket on Keeping Up Appearances.

. . .

I know my grandmother holds Ireland close to her. Although she is the last alive out of her siblings, she still has a growing family back in Donegal, full of nieces, nephews, and sisters and brothers-in-law. She goes back to visit often, usually once a year with Pop Pop and my aunt. Although I have yet to visit, I get a piece of Ireland whenever I see my grandmother. Sometimes, when my sister and I were in the car with Mom Mom we'd ask her to say something in Gaelic. When we visited her house, we'd see pictures of Mount Errigal and the church she and her family went to. I never used to hear my grandmother's Irish accent until my mother told me she had one. It was then I started to notice the subtle difference in the way she sounded.

I am only a quarter Irish, but my closeness with my grandmother makes me feel a connection to her roots deeper than just blood. Her identity is weaved through mine, not only because she is my relative, but because of her presence in my life. Hearing her stories, knowing her struggle, has taught me so much about the life I have. Knowing her has helped me answer some of the questions I have about myself, about life in general, and about where I am going to be.

. . .

The drive home from Mom Mom's was always calm. Right before we would leave, my aunt or grandmother would stand right by the mailbox and look out to make sure no cars were coming since my dad couldn't see. Once they gave us the thumbs up, Dad whipped the car out once more onto 439. I always looked back to see my aunt or grandmother walking back into the house, illuminated by the setting sun, getting smaller and smaller as we drove away.

. . .

Mom Mom came to the United States on May 1st, 1959,

and still lives here today. She lives in White Hall, Maryland, where my mom and aunt grew up. Her first name is Brigid, like St. Brigid, the patroness of Ireland, a beautiful Saint who gave her life to God and the poor. She has two grandchildren, me and my sister, and continues to write "Mom Mom loves you" on all the cards she sends us on holidays. She is my grandmother, my mother's mother, my family.

18. Discerning What?

Each year I grow older, and consequently, grow a little wiser. Sometimes I look back on past years in my life, wondering how I possibly lived like that and was still happy. I like to think of my life as a ladder, each year a rung, the end of it propped up against a cloud in heaven. I climb up a rung and look down, wondering how I managed to make it this far, while being so far away from God. Sometimes, I think about how I must've been a lame excuse of a Catholic. The best part about looking back at my life, years ahead of the events replaying themselves in my mind, is remembering that I am not there anymore. I've surpassed that rung, and I am one step closer to the light shining forth from the cloud above me.

My biggest fear is not reaching that light. I am afraid that I will fall down that ladder, tumbling down the metal structure just to hit the hard ground with a pathetic splat, never to get up again.

They always tell you that when you're up really high somewhere to never look down. When I'm on that ladder, I do anyway. It's good to look down sometimes, to see how far you've come. But then you see how far you could fall if you slipped a little.

There are times when I feel like I am having an internal war. They are the worst kind, because nothing is happening on the outside, everything is hidden beneath a cordial "hello" or a smile to a stranger. In reality, anxiety is building and bursting at the seams about something that has nothing to do with what you're doing. It's when you know something, but it just doesn't feel right. Like *knowing* God exists, but not *feeling* like He's there at all. Like He's left you, or you're too far gone that there's no going back. You know these things aren't true, but a lot of times emotions don't follow the path you want them to go, derailing to some train of thought that doesn't matter in the long run, but can't help but focusing on it anyway.

In the midst of my spiritual battle, I opened a book that contained the words of St. Catherine of Siena. I didn't know what I was going to read. I opened it to a page that I had previously marked with a pale yellow post-it note, now deteriorating at the edges, the stickiness wearing thin. It was about perfect love. There were a lot of sentences and paragraphs that I didn't understand. I kept reading. I was still falling, after all, and there was nothing left to do.

I never thought about being a nun. Especially now, when that feeling of unworthiness was taking precedent and I couldn't seem to get my hand on a rung for the life of me. Where was God in all this, and did He even want me? How could I possibly join the likes of St. Catherine of Siena, who literally saw visions of God and talked to Him face to face? I couldn't understand the cost of becoming a religious sister to feel just as lost as I already had been.

I don't end up becoming a nun at the end of this. I don't end up with a visitation from the Lord telling me to go to the nearest convent and pick up a habit. I wish discerning a vocation were that easy. That at a certain age we received a message telling us what we're supposed to do with our lives like some Godly Hogwarts letter. The stress of a young person discerning a vocation feels greater than the stress of choosing a career since now we have the weight of choosing God's will on our shoulders. The idea that we have to decide whether or not we get married or join a convent or become a priest or a brother is intimidating. It's a beautiful freedom, but at the same time there's always that thought that I might choose the wrong thing. How could I possibly know what God wants for me? No matter how much I pray the answer just never seems to be there.

I don't think there will ever be a clear answer. Not with the way God likes to work. I'm sure I'll know someday, deep within my heart I'll know. Maybe I'll meet a dreamy man who loves God and then there will be no doubts about it. But on top of choosing the right thing to do, it is doing that right thing in the right way that scares me. Faith is a constant climb up that ladder and I don't think I could ever be satisfied with my vocation at any spot on the ladder. I can't be a good wife or mother if my spiritual life isn't in tip top shape. I can't be a nun if I get distracted during the most basic of prayers. What if there's a day where nothing seems to make sense and I just can't believe? Surely that won't fly in a religious order.

There seems to be a mentality among young Catholic

girls and women (I'm sure some men, too) that we have to be seen as perfect servants of God at every second of the day. That to be good Christians we have to be at the top of our game without fail. Both our hands need to be firmly on the rungs of the ladder and we need to be steadily climbing up without any stumbling or misplacement of the feet.

This perfection mentality is what I have been struggling with since I entered high school. After entering freshman year and accepting my faith in its entirety, I found myself feeling a new kind of pressure creeping up from behind my back, growing each year that I was in school. There were not many devout Catholics at my school and I was really the only outspoken one. There have been many times that I wish I was quiet about my faith. That I kept it wrapped up in a nice, neat, little box that I could open when I got home from school. But I'm very loud and once I start talking I don't stop, so that little box method was not an option. There are many times when I have to feel like I'm at a perfect stage in my faith all the time, since there are so many eyes watching me, at least according to my perception. I feel like I may be the only representation of what a religious person is like and I have to do that justice. There are many times where I feel like I represent the whole Church, and that's just another pressure to put on top of everything.

The uncertainty of the life ahead and the insecurity of being imperfect all come together to create a nice concoction called fear of failure. That's what surrounds all of it. Fear that we choose the wrong path over the one that was meant for us and fear that we don't do it right (or don't look like we're doing it right). The way to make that feeling go away is still a mystery to me. I wish I knew how to become more certain in what I was doing or how I would do it (whatever "it" may be), but for the time being it remains in the unknown. A big "What" surrounding the outside of the answer. To be honest, I don't think other people quite know how to tackle uncertainty and insecurity either, no matter the age.

Like I said, I don't know exactly how to tackle both uncertainty and insecurity when they collide. The perfection mentality constantly tells us that we're not good enough and that to be good enough, we need to make ourselves perfect before the Lord. Even if we try to put our trust in God that human instinct kicks in telling us that there is no way we're moving up that ladder.

There will continue to be that big "What" surrounding uncertainty and insecurity. I hope one day I will have enough strength to fully and completely put my trust in God, ditching that perfection mentality. Until then, I'll keep climbing that ladder, getting closer and closer to what He wants, and farther away from what everybody else wants.

Acknowledgments

To my mother and father: Your constant care for me and unconditional love is the greatest thing I could ever ask for. Thank you for supporting my writing (and everything else) always. I love you.

To my sister, Olivia: Thank you for dealing with me all the time. I don't know how you do it. You are so intelligent, kind, and loving. You never cease to amaze me with your strength, knowledge, and faith. Without you, this book would lose its base.

To the Carver Center Literary Arts Class of 2018: Thank you so much for keeping me accountable, keeping me writing, and always never going easy on me. I will miss all the memories we have created together.

To my cousins, Kristen, Kelsey, Jonny, and Elizabeth (Ryan, too): You guys are great. Our family memories are here in this book, I hope you don't mind, but they were too funny to leave out. Thank you for always being the role models I needed.

To Papaw: Thank you for always being there for me, even now. Your perseverance and dedication inspire me to keep on writing every day. Say hi to JPII for me.

To Nana, Mom Mom, and Pop Pop: Without your hard work and love, I would not have the opportunities I have today. I am so grateful for everything you have done for me. Thank you. I love you.

To Annette: I don't know what I did to deserve you in my life. You give me confidence and hope. This book is for you.

To Angie: Thank you for sticking with me all these years. I am so grateful God sent me you to have as my best friend. I don't know where I would be without your constant guidance and support.

To Lauren Mckeegan, Nicole Acaso, and Kevin Anacta: When I was 11, you three put me on the path towards the loving embrace of God. For that, I am eternally grateful. There are many words in this book that would not have been put on the page without your guidance and love. Thank you Thank you Thank you.

To Mrs. Supplee: Thank you for giving this book the attention and care that it needed. You have given me a space to do nothing but write. I am so grateful for the opportunities that you have given me. Without you, this book would be a big pile of slop.

To Mrs. Mlinek: Words cannot capture how much your influence has impacted my writing. From lessons in journalism to reading Shakespeare and the Romantics, your passion is what has driven me these past three years. I will never forget what you have taught me.

To Caroline: Thank you for creating a beautiful cover that encapsulates my writing. You are so talented. I am so grateful to have someone so wonderful to create the cover for this book.

To the reader: Thank you for reading this book. I hope you never stop reading. Please never stop asking questions.

To the Father, Son, and Holy Spirit: Your eternal grace never ceases to amaze me. All my heart (and this book) belongs to You. When I felt like giving up, when I felt lonely or scared, Your loving and merciful embrace kept me going. All glory and honor to You.

ABOUT THE AUTHOR

Lauren Goodwin lives in Perry Hall, Maryland with her Mother, Father, younger sister Olivia, and her shi-tzu Lily. She attends Carver Center for Arts and Technology in Towson, Maryland, where she studies Literary Arts. Lauren loves playing volleyball, reading everything, and praying. Her favorite genres to write are poetry, creative nonfiction, and journalism and has been working on her school newspaper for three years. When not at her house, you can find her at St. Joseph Catholic Church in Fullerton, her second home. She will attend the Catholic University of America in Washington D.C. in the Fall and hopes to be a Saint one day.

94359337R00114

Made in the USA
Columbia, SC
30 April 2018